C DATA BASE DEVELOPMENT

Al Stevens

MIS: PRESS

MANAGEMENT INFORMATION SOURCE, INC.

COPYRIGHT

DEDICATION

Since 1958, when I saw a computer for the first time, I have worked many places with many people and was often changed by these associations. This book is dedicated to those colleagues who contributed measurably to the quality of my career — sometimes with guidance, often by example, and always through friendship:

Ed Dwyer
Chester Fortune
John Harlow
Dave McElroy
Raymond Aubrey Sears
Pat Thursam
Wild Bill Whelan (The Bayou and other joints)

ACKNOWLEDGMENTS

Thanks are due to these companies who contributed C compilers so that the work in this book could extend to the largest possible audience.

Borland International, Inc., Scotts Valley, CA
Computer Innovations, Inc., Tinton Falls, NJ
Datalight, Seattle, WA
Ecosoft, Inc., Indianapolis, IN
Lattice, Inc., Glen Ellyn, IL
Mark Williams Co., Chicago, IL
MetaWare, Inc., Santa Cruz, CA
Microsoft Corporation, Bellevue, WA
MIX Software, Richardson, TX
The Code Works, Santa Barbara, CA
Whitesmiths, Ltd, Concord, MA
Wizard Systems Software, Inc., Monte Sereno, CA

A special thanks to Ron Herold of PH Associates who has provided encouragement and a continuing user base for much of this software.

TABLE OF CONTENTS

PREFACE

C Data Base Development covers how to use C language to design and develop programs that manage information in a data base. It offers an introduction to the fundamentals of data base management and gives a brief history of how today's data base concepts have evolved. Primarily, however, this book is about how C language is applied in defining a relational data base and implementing the programs needed to process that data.

The text is accompanied by a significant body of source code. This code constitutes a complete relational data base management system, or **DBMS**. With it you can build systems that manage data in the orderly formats known as **data bases**.

In this book, a library of data base management functions is developed in the C language. This library is among the most important of programmer possessions. It is a software tool, and tool building is one of the subjects this book directly addresses.

The subject of tool building was given its first widely read treatment in *Software Tools* by Kernighan and Plaugher (Addison-Wesley, 1976). Although Kernighan is a co-author of *The C Programming Language* (Kernighan & Ritchie, Prentice-Hall, 1978) and Plaugher is president of a company that sells C compilers, *Software Tools* delivers its message not through C but through RATFOR, an effective language that was destined for quiet obscurity. When *Software Tools* was written, no one knew that the world would soon be stormed by the personal computer and that the programming community would navigate through assembly language, BASIC, and PASCAL to settle upon C as the language of choice. Some of the C programmers from those days knew that such a thing *should* happen, but no one guessed that it actually would happen. So *Software Tools* was written with RATFOR. A later edition (1981) was published with the tools written in Pascal, but the work has not been published with C as the toolset's language.

Software Tools emphasizes the stand-alone program as a tool. Examples of these programs are word-counting programs, file-sorting utility programs, and text-indexing programs. *C Data Base Development,* however, takes a different approach to software tool building by emphasizing the use of C language functions as reusable software tools that can be called from your custom applications programs, and, in particular, it emphasizes those functions that serve a common purpose —the management of data bases.

The foundation of tool building is as follows: when you write a program or a function, ask if it could be applied to other applications. If so, write the code to be reusable, and store that code where you can find it when you need it. Later, call the code up and polish it some, perhaps making it even more reusable. Also, seize any opportunity to augment your collection with the tools created by other programmers (within the limits of copyright law, of course). Do all of these steps and before long you will have an impressive tool collection.

The software tool concept is based on the premise that most software systems are built from a set of common components, and those components can be programmed as reusable software modules. The reusable functions that support those common processes are software tools. The more complete your toolset, the fewer programs you will write for each new application. Consider for a moment that many applications systems can be described in terms so general that they cannot be distinguished from many other applications. If you interview programmers for a new job, you will find that the more generally they describe their last assignment, the quicker you will identify with it, and the less you will know about it. If a programmer tells you that he or she designed a system that used a screen driver to collect transactions that were posted against a relational data base, you may not know what the system does, but you might know that you have worked on a dozen other systems that can be similarly described.

To build a tool collection, you must know how to write a reusable function and how to enter it into a library of functions where it is available when you need it again. But, most of all, you must know a potential tool when you see one. Such wisdom should come with experience. After you have written the same function several times, the process will sink in; you should catalog that function to spare yourself the effort of writing it again. After you have had that experience several times, you will learn to look at the functions you are writing to see if they could be reusable tools.

One way to learn to be a software tool builder is through the example of another programmer's collection and experiences. In my first book, *C Development Tools for the IBM PC* (Brady, 1986), I explained how the philosophies of programming are centered in top-down design, bottom-up development, structured programming, information hiding, and software tools, and I provided a library of software functions that set those examples. In this book, I try to teach you more of the fundamentals of software systems and give you more software tools that support these advanced methods.

First came the idea. Then came the tools. Then came the book. The code in this book was not developed so that a book could be written. The code is for developing systems. All the programs were written to support specific programming assignments. You can survive without such programs, but with them, you can become a better programmer.

Programmers have few qualities that allow them to outperform their fellow programmers. Native ability is one. Special knowledge of an application or a technology is another. Techniques for improved programming productivity are still more. Assume you have superior native ability. But look around you: Genius abounds. You will be admired and hired for your achievements, *not* for your I.Q. "What have you done for me lately?" prospective employers and clients will ask. If you are a specialist in some functional application, you will work as long as programs are needed that match your specialty. If you have unique knowledge of a particular language, computer, or operating system, then you will work when someone needs your particular expert skill. But if your specialties are information processing, data structures, data management, user interfaces, and writing working programs, then you will always work because these capabilities are a part of every system; moreover, if you can deliver a system in less time than it ought to take to build one, then you will be in demand. And that fact is true regardless of the language, the operating system, the computer, or the application.

To establish yourself as a programmer who is in demand, you must acquire the knowledge and skill that will make you the productive programmer that clients and employers want to hire. You need to learn how to build acceptable programs for the people who want those programs.

First, learn what passes for good software — not necessarily what constitutes good software, but what passes for it. If the software does what the user wants it to do, then it passes the most critical test. The quality of a new program has no better measure. The customer paying for the software does not usually read the code and cares little about the programming principles or elegant algorithms that the programmer uses. The customer wants the software to work.

Next, learn how a program stays productive. If it holds up — if it is reliable — then it has the first chance to remain a good program. The second chance comes on that infrequent occasion when the program fails. If you or some other programmer can find the problem and fix it without much extra time and agony, then the program is reasonably maintainable and is still a good program. The third chance comes when the user wants to change the function of the program. Remember that the solution to a problem usually modifies the program, and most programs are going to be changed. If a program is modifiable, then it is a good program because you can change it.

Those attributes just listed are marks of a good program. Another mark is its usefulness, which is measurably increased if the program is ready when it is supposed to be. Some programmers regard their programs as works of art, not to be released until the programs are perfect. Perfection, in the view of some software hackers, is in the internals of the program and not in its usefulness. A program in the hands of one of these birds might be aesthetically beautiful and elegantly coded yet totally worthless because it is not available when it is needed.

If you know how to get a reliable, maintainable, modifiable, usable program into the hands of the user on schedule and within budget, there isn't much more you need to know.

This book addresses an area of knowledge that many programmers lack: the understanding of data structures and how to implement them.

In the early days of programming, data structures were constrained by the hardware itself. My first programming job in the late 1950s was with the IBM 650, and the input and output were punched cards and printed listings. The user was the computer operator, and the user interface was a panel of lights and switches. (That old 650 was visited more by the person who replaced vacuum tubes than by the operator.) Our data structures consisted of 80-column punched cards and 120-column printed listings.

When we moved up to tape and disk in the so-called "second generation," the operator had a hard-copy typewriter console and more lights and switches, but we programmers had tape and disk — two new kinds of mass storage to deal with — and we had to start thinking about more complex data structures. We sank to the challenge. We invented data models involving complex header and trailer records loaded with inter-record and inter-file pointers and all kinds of spaghetti logic. Variable-length records were common. Hashing algorithms used strange formulae to compute record addresses from various parts of the data values and provided the techniques for random access. It was usual to have many records hashing to the same address, so we invented collision strategies that involved overflow areas and more pointers and secondary hashing algorithms. Whenever some new requirement would surface, the whole programming staff went into a dither about how much software needed changing; the new wrinkle never seemed to fit into the old data model.

The main problem was that we didn't have a data base management system. We didn't even have file servers. The specific tape and disk read, write, and error correction routines existed in code at the hardware level and were in every program. Disk volumes didn't have file directories; they had files positioned wherever we wanted them, and every program knew the physical sector addresses of the files. If the volume needed reorganizing, scores of programs were changed and retested.

If all that chaos seemed normal, it was because at the time it was. Everyone in the field was going about programming in the same way. Most of us were too busy building systems to stand back and look at the business of building systems. The scholars and researchers sought better ways, however, and the first ideas about general-purpose, reusable software were born. First came device macros that handled input, output, and error checking. Next came the file servers that would find a place for a file and let it grow without involving the applications programs. New ideas poured out. Among them was the notion of the **logical device**, where the program talked to a symbolic device, and the operator assigned the reel of tape or the disk cartridge to a physical device and then mounted it accordingly. That idea matured when operating systems began to translate the program's logical device to a physical device.

Then came the **data base management system (DBMS)**. The idea behind the DBMS was that you could describe an application's data base in a format that was external to the application's programs, and a general purpose software system would tend the data base by adding, deleting, and retrieving records at the request of the programs. From the DBMS came the need for standards for expressing the format of a data base, and from these standards came the idea that most or all data bases could be described from one of a small set of data models.

The development of a common set of data models was strongly influenced by all the wacky and convoluted data structures that programmers had been building for so long. From the disorder came a vision of order. It became apparent that discipline and structure must be applied. Without it, the DBMS would not be possible. The quest for order resulted in the development of three data models: the **hierarchical** model, the **network** model, and the **relational** model. Any data structure problem could be solved with one of these models. (You will find discussions of these data models in Chapter 4.)

At last programmers had some standards to follow. They had to follow them because they were being given these DBMSs to use, and each one would support only one of the models. Programmers could not repeat their past sins with contrived data structures because the tools at hand wouldn't support any of them.

So where does all this development leave us with the personal computer? Do we have the same structural standards for data? Perhaps yes, perhaps no. The proliferation of the little computer spawned a new generation of programmers, and the cycle repeated. When programmers started to build their own computers at home, they didn't build a data base management system to go along with it. The first home-built computers weren't big enough. Besides, programmers considered themselves lucky to get their hands on a BASIC interpreter. Not until these little machines began to get bigger (in power and memory) did programmers get products such as dBASE II that would send them down the correct path. As a result of the lack of such products during the microcomputer's infancy, a generation of homegrown programmers evolved who never learned the lesson of the data model. Consider many of the BASIC programs out there today. Lurking in the hearts of many of these systems are the same kinds of weird data models that the old-timers used to build before anyone knew better.

Times are changing. If a programmer is to produce software systems that are reliable, maintainable, and modifiable, that programmer must know how to build a data base from accepted data structure techniques. Hacked-out solutions are not acceptable any more. Those paying the bills have come to expect better.

It is my belief that the IBM PC has done more to advance the understanding of computer programming than any other computer. It created a consumer base where one did not exist, and, in doing so, created a new generation of programmers. It took the primary programmer's tool —the computer —out of the air-conditioned, raised-floor environment and put it on kitchen tables where programmers could get at it when they wanted to. Because of the new consumers' overwhelming acceptance of the PC, the new programmers are motivated to write programs that will sell. Because of the open architecture of the PC's video display, keyboard, and interrupt structure, programmers can allow their creative imaginations to explore the machine. From these explorations come excursions into different software techniques, and these experiments find their way into consumer programs. The consumers buy what they like, and we learn what to build.

But knowing what to build and knowing how to build it are two very different concepts.

Al Stevens
Merritt Island, Florida
May 1987

CHAPTER 1

INTRODUCTION

1 Introduction

The software in this book consists of functions that the programmer includes in a software system, which, in turn, are tools that become part of the total application once it is operational. By supporting requirements that are common among most systems, the functions reduce the amount of code you must write when you are developing a new application. These tools represent a layer of software that sits between the custom application code and hardware and the operating system. As such, they provide support to higher levels of common system requirements and reduce the quantity of code you develop. When you use proven and reliable utility code — or software tools — instead of writing one-of-a-kind custom functions, your software system gains a significant measure of reliability.

Programming should include the philosophy and disciplines of portable software, top-down design, bottom-up development, structured programming, information hiding, and, above all, reusable software tool building. These measures are sound, and they will serve you well if you remain faithful to their principles.

If you develop software tools that can be ported to different computers, you are, through your portable tool collection, a more productive programmer. Some programmers go from assignment to assignment without taking as much as a program listing. The work they do in each assignment remains behind, and they start a new project with only their skill and knowledge. Perhaps with the example of a useful tool collection, they could have learned to build reusable software to carry over to future applications. This book can set that example.

You will find plenty of books about C on the Computer Science shelves in bookstores. But even though most of them serve useful purposes, they seem to fall short of the mark when it comes to providing useable C functions. Many don't shoot for that particular mark, but the ones that do seem to miss.

A typical book explains the C language and provides examples of how to use its features. Some books provide simple functions to illustrate algorithms and the language principles. Often, the functions are similar to those available in the libraries of compilers. More often, they are textbook examples without much practical use. An author needs to deliver his message in as brief and concise a manner as possible. Not only are large software systems difficult to publish —because of the size of the source files —but they are difficult to explain. Complex algorithms need simple explanations, and comprehensible discussions of intricate subjects are difficult to develop. Even so, the objective of this book is to provide complete, useful software tools —tools that you can put to work in the next software system you develop and that are easy to use and understand. You will be able to actually use the software published here, and you will be able to apply it and your new knowledge in developing data base systems.

To use this book, you need a programmer's understanding of the IBM PC and the PC-DOS software development environment. You need to understand the DOS hierarchical file structure and the associated paths and file directories and subdirectories. And you need to know how PC-DOS batch files work. Several good texts are available that will teach you this infomation. If you have been programming the IBM PC to any extent at all, you might already be familiar with some of them. Two that are recommended are *The Peter Norton Programmer's Guide to the IBM PC* (1985) by Peter Norton and *Advanced MS-DOS* (1986) by Ray Duncan, both published by Microsoft Press. You should keep these two books handy whenever you are writing programs that reach beyond the standard C function library.

This book does not attempt to teach you how to program in C; instead, it assumes that you are already a C programmer. Perhaps you could install this software without ever learning the basics of the C language, but you would never be able to use the functions for anything beyond the applications examples published here. Even though the examples are functional and useful software packages, they themselves are not the point of this book. Their purpose is to illustrate the use of the toolset functions; if you can use the examples as applications, then all the better. But you need more. Two elements essential to a productive programming career are an understanding of software tool building as a discipline and a collection of software tools to use. If this collection shows you by example that tool building is a good idea, the first purpose of this book has been successful. If you can use the tools in your work, the second purpose has been realized.

Perhaps the functions published here will be a significant addition to your personal library of software tools. If so, the book has met its objective. If that addition turns out to be a starter set — if you have not yet begun tool building — then the book has served an even greater purpose because you are about to become a better programmer.

DATA BASE MANAGEMENT

The data base management system found in later chapters is written as generic software that you can move into many environments without undue concern for the hardware or operating system used. The package has worked on several varieties of computers, ranging from the Z80 to the 80286 microprocessors, under four operating systems: PC-DOS, CP/M-80, CP/M-86, and TurboDos. This system has come together into a single package that operates on the IBM PC under IBM PC-DOS but is portable to other environments. The PC version is published in this book.

CHAPTER OVERVIEWS

Chapters 2 through 8 address the data base and the data base management system (DBMS) that supports the software applications you develop. These chapters include a library of functions that, when called from your applications programs, provide most of the facilities of a DBMS. With this knowledge and the toolset, you can write software systems that process data organized in the **relational** model. The relational data base theory is discussed in Chapter 4.

Chapter 2 explains data base principles by addressing each of the components of data that constitutes a data base. It then proceeds to show how you describe a data base by using a language known as the **data base schema**. You will learn to design data bases as logically interrelated files, each containing data elements, and to index the records in the files by the values of chosen data elements called **keys**. You will then see how the data element dictionary is the basis for all related data definitions.

Chapter 3 discusses how to design a data base from scratch. You can build a data base design by collecting the requirements for data storage and by taking an inventory of the data items that must be stored and retrieved.

Chapter 4 addresses the DBMS itself, the system of software that supports your data by providing functions to describe the architecture of the data base, to store and retrieve records in response to calls from your programs, and to maintain the integrity and continuity of the indices into the record contents. This chapter contains the essence of this book's DBMS approach and assumes that the reader has a moderate knowledge of C syntax.

Chapter 5 discusses the features of the C programming language as they apply to the definition of a data base. The technique described allows you to change the data format without concern for most of the software that processes it.

Chapter 6 introduces the "Cheap Data Base Management System," called **Cdata**. With Cdata you develop the specifications of a data base by using the techniques addressed in Chapter 5. This subject is followed by a discussion of Cdata's data manipulation language functions. You use these functions to store and retrieve records to and from the data base.

Chapter 7 presents a series of utility functions to manipulate data in the data base. These functions include programs to enter data into the file records, retrieve records by indexed key data elements, and generate reports based on data records retrieved from the data base. Chapter 7 also includes a schema compiler program that reads a tabular description of the data base schema from a text file and generates the Cdata data definition language described in Chapter 6.

Chapter 8 presents an example of a complete — although small — software system that builds a consultant's billing system with the Cdata DBMS.

Finally, Chapter 9 explains how you can build the software published in this book by using one of the compilers. The procedure for each compiler accompanies an appropriate PC-DOS batch file to build the toolset functions and the example applications.

THE C COMPILERS

The software in this book has been installed with nine different C compilers for the IBM PC:

- Aztec C
- Computer Innovations C86
- Datalight C
- Eco-C88
- Lattice C
- Let's C
- Microsoft C
- Turbo C
- Wizard C

The discussions that follow do not judge the compilers against one another. They all work, and they are all excellent products. Each compiler has its strengths and weaknesses. If you have one of them, then you can use this software, and it will work. If you have a different compiler and it supports the full C language, then the conversion should be smooth. The conversion of C programs between compilers was once a tough job; the language standard had not settled in, the compilers were different, and most programmers were inexperienced in the issues of portability. But with time and experience the problems of portability have diminished. Each change that was made to this book's software to move it to the next compiler resulted in more consistent, portable code. This multiple-compiler exercise resulted in an appreciation of the need for a standard C dialect. Fortunately, the compilers are converging on a standard language, and programmers are becoming sensitive to the problems of writing portable code.

This software works with nine different compilers. But at least seven other C compilers are available for the IBM PC:

- C-Systems C
- DeSmet C
- Digital Research C
- High C
- Mix C
- QC88
- Whitesmiths' C

You might wonder why a computer needs sixteen different compilers (and nearly as many interpreters) for the same language. What other language boasts so many compilers that are actively and successfully marketed for the same computer and the same operating system? The popularity of C among programmers and its natural compatibility with the architecture of the personal computer account for the success of such a significant number of compilers. Large software companies have added to the C mania by choosing it as their development language. Software written in C is more readily converted to other computers and operating systems than software developed in other languages. This portability is the most touted feature of C and is one good reason for its popularity. Software companies like to react quickly to changes in trends in the computer industry. Portable software gives those companies that ability. C gives them portable software.

SUMMARY

The functions in this book are useful, informative, and interesting programs. But, best of all, they are fun. Developing tools for fellow programmers is an ideal assignment for a programmer because it embraces a kindred clientele. A long programming career will know many different user communities, but most programmers don't understand what their users do for a living; however, they do know the pains and pleasures of the programmer's lot. Some have known them through several generations of computers and have waded through many iterations of discovering and rediscovering the principles and practices of their craft. It is hoped that you will find as much enjoyment in studying and using these programs as the author has found in developing them.

CHAPTER 2

DATA BASE FUNDAMENTALS

The next three chapters discuss the principles of data base architecture and design and the data base management system (DBMS). If you are an experienced data base analyst, you might want to skip these chapters, but you are encouraged to read them all. Although none of the three is comprehensive, together they can help you understand the software presented in the remainder of the book because they reveal a perspective of data base theory that may differ from your own. Many "standards" of the software industry are defined and redefined by popular use rather than by studied application. When a technical phrase such as "relational data base" becomes fashionable, its meaning can be lost when those who do not know its original definition use it extensively. Zealous advertising, uninformed media treatment, and layperson involvement can result in the unintended redefinition of a phrase.

The job of a system designer/developer is complex. His or her objective is to produce a useful automated system. To do this, the designer must provide for an orderly, disciplined definition of the system's components. An automated system contains many elements or subsystems including requirements analyses, hardware, software, user and operator documentation, maintenance, and training.

This book is about software. Software consists of programs and information; good programs need information to process, and information requires effective processing to be useful. To make information suitable for processing, you must organize it into a disciplined and consistent form called a **data base**.

In this chapter, a data base is defined, and a small personnel data base is presented as an example. Chapter 3 explains the process of data base design and uses the example personnel data base to illustrate the steps taken in its design. Chapter 4 explains the data base management system and how to build the data base design into the software system that will manage it.

THE DATA BASE

Definition:

*A **data base** is an integrated collection of automated data files related to one another in the support of a common purpose.*

Each file in a data base is made of **data elements**—account numbers, dates, amounts, quantities, names, addresses, hat sizes, and many other identifiable items of data. These data elements are to be organized by, stored in, and retrieved from the data base. To design such a data base, you must understand files, their data elements, and how they are used.

To a designer, data means automated information, i.e., information in a format acceptable for automatic processing by a computer. Information can be automated when it can be reduced into a machine-readable form.

The smallest component of data in a computer is the **bit**, a binary element with the values of 0 and 1. Programmers are sometimes concerned with bits but, as the data base designer, you will view data from a higher perspective. Bits are used to build **bytes** (or characters), which are used to build data elements. Data files contain **records** that are made up of data elements, and a data base consists of **files**. Take time to learn the hierarchy of data in a data base because it figures significantly in the rest of this book. Starting from the highest level, the hierarchy is as follows:

1. data base
2. file
3. record
4. data element
5. character (byte)
6. bit

At this stage in the design, the first five levels in the hierarchy are of primary interest. The data base contains files of records that contain data elements made up of characters.

Figure 2.1 shows a popular analogy to the data base—the office file drawer. The drawer represents the data base, the folders represent the files, the documents in the folder represent the records, and the information on the documents represents the data elements. The analogy is so popular that some data base systems use file cabinets, drawers, and folders as video icons (small graphic pictures) to represent components of the data base.

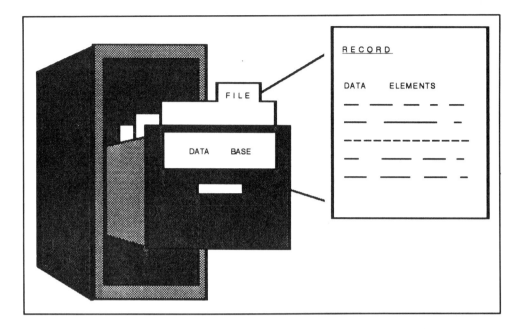

Figure 2.1   The Data Base Analogy

The analogy is not perfect, however. The paper records stored in file drawers are usually done so without strict discipline. Of course, an efficient file clerk attempts to maintain order, but his or her attention provides the only control. In an automated data base, the controls are designed into the data base and the software. Each item of data serves a specific purpose, and information is not unnecessarily repeated. Everything needed is there, and anything that does not fit is not allowed. The records in a file all have the same format, with identical sets of data elements in all records in the same file.

To design a data base, you must understand data structures and interrelationships. The document (record) in a folder (file) has form and structure, and the folder contains many copies of the same document with different information (data values) filled into the blank entry spaces (data elements) of the document. The many folders are collected in a drawer (data base), representing the collection of information. The file cabinet itself is analogous to the total information resource of an organization.

Now, begin to understand data base by examining the lowest addressable item of automated data — the data element.

THE DATA ELEMENT

Data bases are filled with items of information. The values these items contain need places to be stored. The repository for a piece of data is called the **data element**.

Definition:

A data element is a place in a file used to store an item of information that is uniquely identifiable by its purpose and contents.

The data element has functional relevance to the application being supported by the data base. Examples of data elements are dates, account numbers, amounts, quantities, names, addresses, phone numbers, and batting averages. Their functional relationship to the application's purpose is important: a data element is recorded in a data base because it contributes to the context of the functions supported by the system. For example, the salary of an employee is a relevant data element in a payroll system, while the item quantity on hand is relevant in an inventory system. Either data element would seem to be misplaced in the other system.

The data element is the temporary home for a transient value of information. Do not confuse the data element (the place for the data to be stored) with the **data value** (the current contents of the data element). The employee record will always contain the data element for the employee's salary, but that data element will have different values for different employees, and the value for a given employee will change from time to time.

Definition:

A data value is the information stored in a data element.

The Data Element Dictionary

A data base design task often begins with the development of a list of data elements. Whether or not you begin with such a list, you should eventually create one. The following table is an example of a list of data elements for a small personnel system data base. This example illustrates the foundation of data base design — the **data element dictionary.**

Data Element Name	Data Type	Length
employee__no	numeric	5
employee__name	alphanumeric	25
date__hired	date	6
salary	currency	10
dept__no	numeric	5
dept__name	alphanumeric	25
proj__no	numeric	5
proj__name	alphanumeric	25
start__date	date	6
completion__date	date	6
labor__budget	numeric	5
hours__charged	numeric	5

The data element dictionary is central to the application of the data base management tools presented in this book. You must define all data items that appear on screens, reports, and in data files in the data element dictionary. An exception to this rule is the constant, literal information used on screens and reports for report titles and input prompting messages. You do not need to define data elements for this information, although some data base management systems do not distinguish such information from real data elements.

Definition:

A data element dictionary is a table of data elements including at least the names, data types, and lengths of every data element in the subject data base.

Data Element Types

The data element dictionary just shown includes names, types, and lengths of the elements. The types are from the following list:

Date
Currency
Numeric
Alphanumeric

These element types are not the only ones you might use, but you can describe any data element in a commercial application with one of these types. Other generic data element types are phone number, zip code, state, social security number, and so on. The extent to which you can support generic data element types varies from system to system. One of the most popular (and expensive) mainframe data base management systems allows you to define data elements as numeric or alphanumeric only, allowing no more specific generic types. Often, generic data element types are insufficient to describe data without further definition. Some generic types imply form and function, but the implication is not rigid. The implied format of a date or a phone number seems obvious, but you will encounter any of several formats for these two simple types. Consider the following examples:

Telephone numbers	Dates
(202)555-1212	01/02/86
PE 6-5000	3 Jan 64
Dial 'M' for Myrtle	The Ides of March

Data Element Names

The names of data elements in data element dictionaries are used by programs and users to identify the data elements. They are chosen to describe the function and purpose of the data elements they name. If you have the common programmer's bent for cryptic and short data element names, you are encouraged to reconsider that practice. In a data base management system built from the tools in this book, the data element name is seen by the user and programmer alike. It must be readable by humans as well as machines.

C language data identifiers are used as data element names. These identifiers are unique to the first 31 characters, providing sufficient room for a descriptive name. Chapter 5 explains how to apply this technique.

Data Value Representation

Data elements in a data base will often exploit the data types of the computer or language to preserve storage space or time. You might find a mix of binary integers, floating point numbers, strings, and bit flags combined in the same file. In this book's approach to data storage, all data element values are stored as null-terminated strings. This practice has advantages. The data can be viewed from system utilities that display file data on the screen (TYPE, DUMP, etc.). The use of ASCII character strings allows the data formats and the programs that process them to be portable between computers with different internal data formats. You need not worry that the language or the operating system will treat a particular bit pattern as something inappropriate, such as an end-of-file mark.

FILES

A data base contains a group of files related to one another by a common purpose. Do not confuse the **file** and the **record**. The file is a collection of records. The records are alike in format, but each record is unique in content; therefore, the records in a file all have the same data elements but different data element values.

Definition:

A file is a set of records where the records have the same data elements in the same format.

You can derive the format of a record from a list of data elements that appear in the file.

The organization of the file provides functional storage of data related to the purpose of the system that the data base supports. Interfile relationships are based on the functional relationships of their purposes. To describe a file, give it a name and supply a list of data elements. The name should relate to the purpose of the file, just as the name of a data element describes the data in the element. If you are designing an employee file, it makes sense to call the file something like "EMPLOYEES." Following is an example of how you might describe the file:

> EMPLOYEES:
> employee__no, employee__name, date__hired, salary

If you refer to the data element dictionary for the lengths of the data elements, you can see that the sum of the lengths of the elements in EMPLOYEES is equal to 46 characters. C language terminates strings of data with null-value bytes, so you must add one character to the length of each data element, bringing the total to 50, which is how long a record in the EMPLOYEES file will be.

The Data Base Schema

When designing a data base, you must prepare a formal statement of the files and the format of each file. The techniques for preparing this statement vary according to the style preferred by the developer, but such statements must include at least the files, their data elements, the data elements in each file used to identify specific records, and the implied relationships between files. This description of a data base is called the **schema.**

Definition:

A schema is the expression of the data base in terms of the files it stores, the data elements in each file, the key data elements used for record identification, and the relationships between files.

The small data base used in these discussions is a **relational** data base. The techniques for record indexing and file-to-file relationships are taken from the relational theory of data base management. Other models of data are available, and the data models you might use are discussed in Chapter 4. Since this book includes data base management software and because that software supports the relational model, these discussions lean in that direction.

The Specification of Data Files

As explained previously, a data base is a collection of files. If you understand what constitutes a file, you can consider the components of a data base. In its simplest form, a data base is a set of files that share a purpose. The personnel system example can be expanded to illustrate this point. Including the file named EMPLOYEES defined earlier, the data base (now named PERSONNEL) might consist of these files:

```
PERSONNEL:
EMPLOYEES:        employee__no, employee__name,
                  date__hired, salary
DEPARTMENTS:      dept__no, dept__name
PROJECTS:         proj__no, proj__name, start__date,
                  completion__date, labor__budget
```

The translation of a schema into a data base management software system usually involves using a language to describe the schema to the data base management software. This language is sometimes called the **data definition language**. In this book's approach to data base definition, the facilities of the C language will be used to build a data definition language, as discussed in Chapter 4.

A schema contains two more data constructs to complete the data base design: the individual file index key specifications and the interfile relationships.

Key Data Elements

The records in every file must be uniquely identified so the system can find and retrieve each one. You need a way to tell the computer which record to retrieve, and the computer needs to know how to find a requested record. Some file management systems allow you to retrieve a record by calling out its position in the file or record number, but this method isn't adequate. You don't want to remember where a record is stored, just that it is in the file and available to you. It is, however, reasonable to expect you to remember something about the data in the record you want to retrieve. Given what you tell the computer about the data, the computer can find the record by searching for one that contains the provided data value.

The **definition** of a file includes the specification of the data element or elements that are the key to the file. A file **key** logically points to the record that it indexes.

Since a key is an index into the file, that approach is used with data base management tools. With indexed data elements, more than one key can be assigned to a file, which means that you can retrieve a record based on the values of several data elements. Even so, the file will usually have a single, unique key that differentiates each record from all others in the file. This key is called the **primary key** because only one record in a file can contain a given value of a primary key.

Definition:

*The **primary key data element** in a file is the data element used to uniquely describe and locate a desired record. The key can be a combination of more than one data element.*

In the example EMPLOYEES file, the "employee_no" data element is the primary key. Nonprimary keys that index a file are **secondary keys**, and more than one record can contain the same value. Initially, just identify the primary data elements for the files in the PERSONNEL data base. To do this, the data base schema will be repeated with the primary key data element underlined in each file.

PERSONNEL:
EMPLOYEES: <u>employee no</u>, employee_name,
                date_hired, salary
DEPARTMENTS: <u>dept no</u>, dept_name
PROJECTS: <u>proj no</u>, proj_name, start_date,
                completion_date, labor_budget

You can find employee records if you know the employee number. Similarly, department records are keyed on the department number, and the project number indexes the project file.

Interfile Relationships

The schema developed for the PERSONNEL data base does not show how the files are related. The ability to maintain the relationships between files is one of the strengths of a data base management system. Files are related when a data record in one file associates with a data record in another file. When employees are assigned to projects, the record for employee Oppenheimer (in the EMPLOYEES file) could be related to the record for the Manhattan project (in the PROJECTS file). It is not necessary that all employees be assigned projects or that all projects have employee assignments for the relationship to exist between the files. You could have a lot of employees, a lot of projects, and no project assignments, and the relationship would still exist if the data base design provided for the potential assignment of employees to projects. In the example of the PERSONNEL data base, no potential is shown for files to be related, but that capability will be added to the data base schema next.

In a data base, you can relate one file to another in one of three ways:

- one-to-one
- many-to-one
- many-to-many

Consider the relationships involved in the records of teachers and students. When students hire full-time tutors to better learn a subject, a one-to-one relationship occurs between a file of tutors and a file of students; a tutor has just one student and a student has just one tutor. A data base that supports the tutor-to-student relationship will be said to support a one-to-one relationship between the two files. Even though the data base has many students and many tutors, the relationship is one-to-one because each tutor or student has only one of the other.

In elementary school, one teacher has many students, and each student has only one teacher. This constitutes a one-to-many relationship.

In high school and college, a teacher teaches many students, and each student has many teachers. This is an example of a many-to-many relationship.

Figure 2.2 uses this example to illustrate how relationships between teachers and students can be depicted. To design a data base with teacher-student relationships, you would start with a chart similar to one of the three parts of Figure 2.2. Each oval represents a file and each connecting arrow represents an interfile relationship. The arrows have single and double arrowheads connecting the files. A single arrowhead points to a "to-one" relationship; a double arrowhead points to a "to-many" relationship.

Figure 2.3 shows the relationships in the PERSONNEL data base, using the arrowhead symbols.

Each department works on only one project, and each project belongs to only one department; therefore, the relationship between the DEPARTMENTS file and the PROJECTS file is one-to-one.

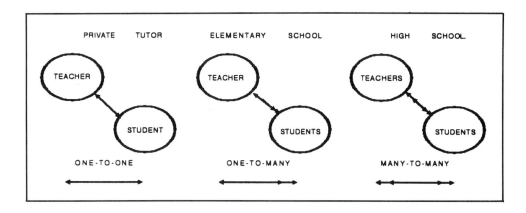

Figure 2.2   The Three Relationships

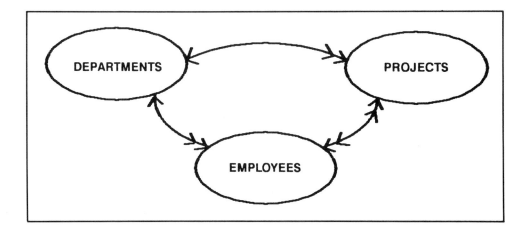

Figure 2.3   The PERSONNEL Data Base

A department employs more than one employee, and an employee can work for only one department, so the relationship of the DEPART-MENTS file to the EMPLOYEES file is one-to-many. Conversely, the EMPLOYEES file has a many-to-one relationship with the DEPART-MENTS file.

A project has more than one employee assigned to it, and an employee can work on many projects, so the EMPLOYEES file and the PROJECTS file have many-to-many relationships with each other.

The technique for describing these relationships is not complicated. A file has a primary key data element. If another file has a many-to-one relationship with this file, the other file includes (among its data elements) the primary key data element of the first file. Following is the PERSONNEL data base schema with key elements in the files where the relationships exist:

    PERSONNEL:
    EMPLOYEES: employee__no, employee__name,
                        date__hired, salary, **dept__no**
    DEPARTMENTS: dept__no, dept__name
    PROJECTS: proj__no, proj__name, start__date,
                        completion__date, labor__budget,
                        dept__no

Notice that the data element **dept__no** has been added to the EMPLOYEES file and the PROJECTS file. As a result, these files have a many-to-one relationship with the DEPARTMENTS file. Suppose that the relationship between departments and projects is one-to-one. You can use two techniques to support this relationship: concatenating (physically bonding) the two records into one or enforcing the one-to-one circumstance with the applications software that adds records to the PROJECTS file. A record addition is not permitted if another project is already assigned to the department.

Both approaches have their disadvantages, however. The first approach requires that all department records have space for project data, even when the department has no projects. The second approach requires the applications software to enforce the relationship. This approach has potential for loss of data integrity due to careless programming; it works better if the data base design includes inherent integrity constraints that a program cannot violate. Which approach you choose will depend on the problem at hand and the relative merits of each approach for your applications.

Figures 2.4 and 2.5 illustrate how to build the one-to-many relationship. The two files become related when you place **dept__no** — the primary key to the DEPARTMENTS file — in the EMPLOYEES records as a data element. Subsequently, each EMPLOYEES record can point to one DEPARTMENTS record, and, since more than one EMPLOYEES record can point to a DEPARTMENTS record, the design supports the one-to-many relationship. Figure 2.5 shows the two files with data values in the records. (Observe that while two of the EMPLOYEES records (employee__no.'s 00002 and 00005) contain the same **dept__no** (0020), no EMPLOYEES record can relate to multiple DEPART-MENTS records.)

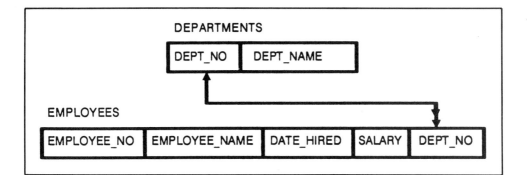

Figure 2.4   **DEPARTMENTS and EMPLOYEES: One-to-Many**

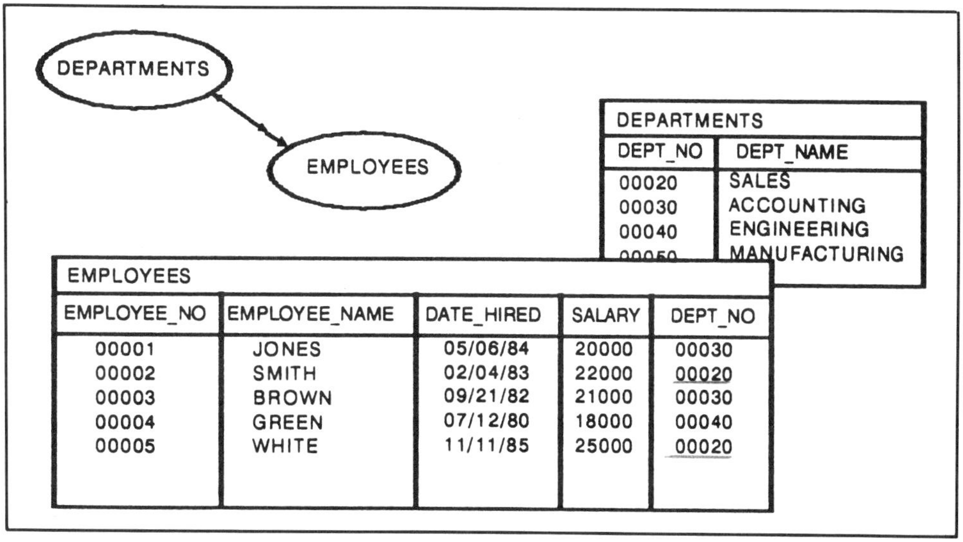

Figure 2.5   Forming the One-to-Many Relationship

There is still one relationship to establish. The PROJECTS file and the EMPLOYEES file have a <u>many-to-many</u> relationship, which is not as easy to build as the other relationships. At first glance, you might think that you could put the **proj__no** data element in the EMPLOYEES file and the **employee__no** data element in the PROJECTS file, but this will not work because a project could point to an employee that points to a different project. Instead, you must build an additional file that has the primary function of maintaining the relationship. <u>This is called a file of **connector** records because the records in the new file effect a logical connection between the records in two other files</u>. Usually, however, you can find additional functional purposes for the file beyond its role as a connector for the other two files. Information often exists that is relevant to the relationship but is without meaning when applied to one of the two participants. For example, in the relationship between employees and projects, you may want to record the hours each employee spent on each project. The expanded schema, with its new file for employee-project assignments, now looks like the following:

```
PERSONNEL:
EMPLOYEES:        employee no, employee_name,
                  date_hired, salary, dept_no
DEPARTMENTS:      dept no, dept_name
PROJECTS:         proj no, proj_name, start_date,
                  completion_date, labor_budget,
                  dept_no
ASSIGNMENTS:      employee no, proj no, hours_charged
```

Notice that the **employee_no** and **proj_no** data elements are underlined. These two items are concatenated into the primary key of the
file because both items are required to uniquely describe a record. The
file can contain many records with the same employee and many
records with the same project, but only one record can have a given
combination of **employee_no** and **proj_no**.

Figures 2.6 and 2.7 are examples of many-to-many relationships. In
Figure 2.6, the PROJECTS and EMPLOYEES files are unchanged from
the earlier schema, which supported no relationships. The addition of
the ASSIGNMENTS file to the schema provides the ability to account
for hours charged by each employee to each project. In addition, it supports the many-to-many relationship between PROJECTS and
EMPLOYEES. The ASSIGNMENTS file has a many-to-one relationship with each of the PROJECTS and EMPLOYEES files because it
has their primary keys as data elements. So a given ASSIGNMENTS
record can point to one PROJECTS record and one EMPLOYEES
record. Further, a record in either of the PROJECTS or EMPLOYEES
files can be pointed to by many ASSIGNMENTS records. The many-to-
many relationship is built through these 2 one-to-many relationships.
From a given EMPLOYEE record, you can find all the ASSIGN-
MENTS records that point to it by extracting the ASSIGNMENTS
records containing the pertinent **employee_no**. Then, you can derive
the many PROJECTS related to the EMPLOYEE by using the
proj_no(s) from the ASSIGNMENTS records. Conversely, the many
EMPLOYEES related to a PROJECT can be determined with a similar
retrieval through the ASSIGNMENTS file.

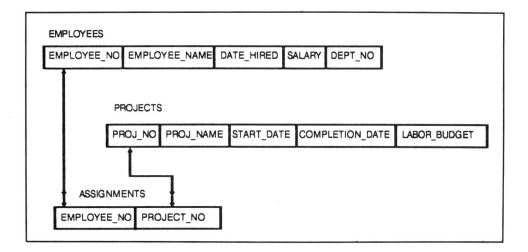

Figure 2.6   EMPLOYEES and PROJECTS: Many-to-Many

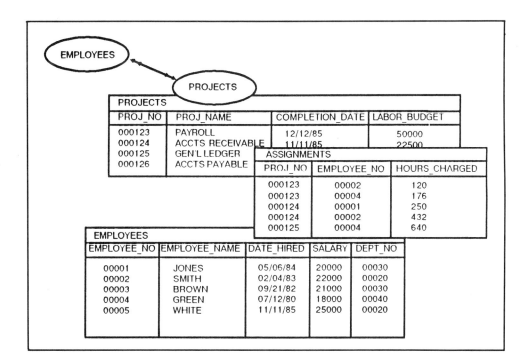

Figure 2.7   Forming the Many-to-Many Relationship

Figure 2.7 shows the three files as they might look with data values included. You can see how the ASSIGNMENTS file associates the 00123 **proj__no** with **employee__no**(s) 00002 and 00004, and **employee__no** 00004 with **proj__no**(s) 00123 and 00125. Thus, a many-to-many relationship is maintained through the connector properties of the ASSIGNMENTS file.

These three relationships are the only ones you need to be concerned with. Anything you might ever want to store in a data base can be stored and maintained using one of these three models.

SUMMARY

This chapter described a data base and discussed its components. The next chapter addresses the often misunderstood and frequently overstated process of designing a data base from scratch.

CHAPTER 3

DESIGNING A DATA BASE

The discussions so far have covered what a data base is, what its component parts are, and how they are related. From these lessons, it is assumed that you would now recognize a data base if you saw one. But how do you design one from scratch? It isn't enough that you have seen a lot of data bases. You can recognize a car when you see one, but you probably don't know how to design or build one even though you might see hundreds of them every day. Recognizing a data base and designing one are two different abilities. Now that you can identify one when you come across it, you need to develop that understanding into an ability to design a working, useful data base from the requirements for a particular application.

Data base design for years has been the coveted domain of a privileged few, those enigmatic gurus who practice the mystic arts of data base administration in the shrines of corporate MIS directorates. Such persons have held sway over the information resources of their benefactors for most of the last twenty-five years. Why? Because only they knew how to design and maintain a data base.

All that elitism is changing. Traditionally, the tools of data base administration were available only where they could be afforded. The big computer and the data base management software were large, expensive, and difficult to get at. No more. The past five years have seen a revolution in the availability of computing power. Users no longer rely on the MIS manager and staff of programmers and data base wizards to bring them the power of computing. The desktop PC is now commonplace, and people are developing their own software.

This chapter explores the basics of data base design, without getting into some of the arcane disciplines that are often advanced as proper design methodology. No myths are exploded, but an idea is put forth that might surprise some data processing seers: anyone can design a workable data base by using intuition and common sense and without applying the mysteries of data base administration.

You won't need special forms, templates, rigid rules, or disciplined procedures for design review and refinement. Those procedures are for the big development project with a big system, a big staff, a big problem to solve, structured management, and the need to avert blame when something goes wrong. They are not necessary for the successful design of a data base, but they are often required by those who find comfort in such things.

You do need a clear understanding of the problem you are trying to solve, of the solutions you might consider, of the ways to translate the solutions into a data base design, and you must be willing to modify the solution as it evolves.

THE NINE STEPS OF DATA BASE DESIGN

The design of a relational data base involves nine steps taken, for the most part, in succession:

1. Identify the basis for the data base requirements
2. Define the data base functional and performance requirements
3. Identify the data items
4. Separate the data elements from the files
5. Build the data element dictionary
6. Gather data elements into files
7. Identify the retrieval characteristics of each file
8. Identify the relationships between files
9. Develop the schema for the DBMS you are using.

There is always a tenth step, which is to reiterate the first nine. Let the solution to the problem modify the problem, and let each successive solution enhance your understanding of the problem. As it does, retrace your steps through the design process, and change your results. This step is called **refinement**, and it is often left out.

The nine steps will now be examined in some detail, using the PERSONNEL data base described as an example in Chapter 2.

IDENTIFY THE BASIS FOR THE DATA BASE REQUIREMENTS

If you are about to design a data base, you must have a mission and a purpose. Someone has asked you to automate something. How was that request made? How much was known about the problem when the solution was requested? Is the problem being solved now? Is the present solution automated or not? Has anyone ever solved a similar problem in a different environment? You need to define the functional and performance requirements for the data base, and the definition of these requirements should proceed from understanding the functions to be supported. You start by identifying the basis of that understanding.

The basis for a data base specifies the problem that is to be solved, the availability of resources that can be used in the solution, and some likely approaches to the solution.

The problem specification can be as simple as a one-line statement of objectives, or it can be a multi-volume report.

Now recall the personnel data base from Chapter 2. Its completed design resembles the following:

```
PERSONNEL:
EMPLOYEES:        employee__no, employee__name,
                  date__hired, salary, dept__no
DEPARTMENTS:      dept__no, dept__name
PROJECTS:         proj__no, proj__name, start__date,
                  completion__date, labor__budget,
                  dept__no
ASSIGNMENTS:      employee__no,__proj__no, hours__charged
```

A problem specification for this data base could be as simple as the one shown here:

Problem: Keep track of the employees within the departments where they work, including their salaries and the date they were hired. Report the status of projects assigned to departments. Record the employees who are working on projects.

The list of available resources includes such information as source documents (employee time cards, for example), interfaces to other data bases, personnel (the sales clerk in a point-of-sale application), and so on. Where appropriate, include examples in the list. The resources list for the personnel data base could resemble the following:

Company Personnel Action Form
Project Work Order
Employee Time Card

Next, an analysis is needed of the possible approaches to the problem. Be as creative and unconventional as you want, but be careful. Make it clear to everyone, including yourself, that these designs are preliminary. Don't make an emotional investment in a premature design, and don't get caught in a situation where someone can hold you to one particular approach.

Your analysis will be influenced by the environment. Perhaps the user already has a computer, so you need not select one. You might be considering the conversion of an existing data base or software system.

To define the basis, start with the present solution. If there is no present solution, start from scratch.

Starting from an Existing Solution

If the user is already using a computer to solve the problem, then you have a good place to start. The existing system will provide insight into the requirements for the data that must be maintained. The user will have experience with an automated solution and will be able to tell you where the new solution can improve on the old. The best way to begin building a new outhouse is to look at an old outhouse. An existing system is an excellent basis for a data base design.

If the user works with a manual system, you would start there. You must collect the functions that the system supports and turn them into a set of requirements for a data base, which will be discussed in more detail later. A manual system will contain enough information to allow you to design an automated one to replace it. As such, it is a good basis for your design. If the purpose of automation is to improve the system's performance, functionality, or both, then the basis will be extended to include the improvements.

Starting from Scratch

It is hard to imagine designing a data base from scratch with no prior procedure for a model. Almost everything has been either automated or set up as a manual procedure. If a user comes to you with the idea of initiating a complete new procedure and solving a brand new problem, you should look around for an existing solution to a similar problem. Chances are someone has already developed the solution you want — or one like it. If you find one, proceed as if you had found it with the new user. If you do not find one, you must start from scratch. The best approach is to develop some manual procedures, use them for a while, and allow them to influence the basis for a new data base. If you cannot do that, you must work with the user to develop an initial basis. Be advised that all of the design and implementation that you do will no doubt change as the data base takes form and is used. You rarely see the best solution the first time.

Write Down the Basis

Once you have the basis for your data base, write it down as you would write a report or a letter. Make it understandable to anyone who understands the problem. Keep your written information around while the system is being developed, and make updates to it as the basis for the system changes. The basis is your foundation for the requirements analysis discussed next.

DEFINE THE DATA BASE
FUNCTIONAL AND PERFORMANCE REQUIREMENTS

This next step is a refinement of the first. From the basis, you define the requirements for the data base. You need to address **functional** requirements and **performance** requirements.

Functional requirements specify the kind of data the data base will contain. In these requirements, you should document everything you know about the functions that are supported. Be specific in identifying pieces of information the data base must know about.

Performance requirements specify frequencies, speeds, quantities, and sizes — how often, how fast, how many, and how big — the data base must support.

The statement of a data base requirement should be clear and unambiguous. It should address itself to one specific aspect of the functions or performance of the system. Each statement should stand alone, and each statement should completely define the requirement. It should be worded so that users and programmers alike can understand it.

Your list of requirements is the planning document for the data base. Anyone who has it and understands it should know what to expect from the system.

Here is an example of a list of requirements that might be developed for the PERSONNEL data base from Chapter 2.

Functional Requirements

1.   The system will record and report the departments in the organization by department number and name.

2.   The system will record and report the organization's employees by employee number. Each employee's record will include the employee's name, salary, and date hired.

3.   The system will record and report the orgranization's projects by project number. Each project's record will include its name, the start and completion dates, and the number of labor hours budgeted to it.

4. The system will record the assignment of employees to departments. An employee is assigned to one department at a time, but a department may have many employees.

5. The system will record the assignment of projects to departments. A project is assigned to one department, and a department may be responsible for many projects.

6. The system will record the assignment of employees to projects. An employee may work on several projects, including projects assigned to departments other than the department to which the employee is assigned. A project may have multiple employees assigned to it.

7. The system will record the hours worked by each employee on each project.

Performance Requirements

1. The system will support up to 10 departments.

2. The system will support up to 100 employees.

3. The system will support up to 20 projects.

4. The system will support up to 200 employee-to-project assignments.

5. Retrieval of data recorded about an employee, project, or department will be on-line and will be in response to the user's entry of the employee, project, or department number. The system will deliver the related data within three seconds of entering the associated control number.

IDENTIFY THE DATA ITEMS

Once you have written down the requirements for the data base, you can begin to translate those requirements into identifiable elements of data that are suitable for automation.

You will need a way to note and organize the data items that you identify. Start with a stack of 3x5 cards, an on-line notepad on your computer, or some other technique that allows you to itemize, sort, and shuffle.

To identify a data item, you must rummage around in the work you have already done, looking for potential data items. From your basis and your requirements, extract every reference to anything that looks like a data item and write its name and anything else you know about that item onto one of your 3×5 cards. You can start by pulling the nouns out of your work. Each noun is a potential data item. The example PERSONNEL system basis and requirements list delivers the following collection of nouns:

> employees, departments, salary, date hired, projects, schedules, hours budgeted, hours worked, department number, department name, employee name, project number, project name, start date, completion date, assignments, hours expended.

This list can be used as an initial collection of the items that will be recorded in and reported from the PERSONNEL system data base you are designing. Of course, as your work proceeds, you will add to and remove from this list.

SEPARATE THE DATA ELEMENTS FROM THE FILES

Here, you apply your designer judgement, intuition, and guesswork. Look at the data items you have collected. Which of these items seem to be individual data elements, and which seem more like logically organized aggregates of data elements? Shuffle them up, sort them out, and move them around. The 3x5 card method works well here. It should become obvious which items are elements and which are not. A date, for example, is clearly a data element. It is not as obvious that an "assignment" is *not* a data element. Can you see how a department number is a data element while a department is a data entity that might be represented by a number of data elements, possibly including the department number?

There is room for confusion here. Some data elements will break down into component parts, leading you to suspect that they might be aggregates. In a typical example, a date can be divided into its month, day, and year. Is each of those pieces of information a data element? Sometimes they can be. Is the date still a data element? Again, sometimes it can be. Your requirements will dictate the level of detail to which an entity of data is defined. If you need to report the "closing day" or the "day placed in service," then you will need to identify these components of a date as separate data elements.

The objective of this exercise is to separate the data elements from the files so that you can take the next two steps. The nouns from the example list above that have been culled out as data elements can be described in this subset of the list:

> salary, date hired, hours budgeted, hours worked, department number, department name, employee name, project number, project name, start date, completion date, hours expended.

BUILD THE DATA ELEMENT DICTIONARY

Recall from Chapter 2 that the data element dictionary is defined and identified as a fundamental component in the design of a data base. Once you have identified what the data elements are, you can build your data element dictionary.

You must collect everything that is known or that can be determined about each data element. At the very least, you will need to know its size and data type. If the design is based on an existing system, the documentation (if any) can contribute to your dictionary. If the documentation is inadequate, but the source code is available, you can "reverse-engineer" the data element characteristics by seeing how the existing software uses them. If you are automating a manual system, you can look at the entry forms (time cards, posting ledgers, and so on) to see how the data elements are used. Sometimes these forms have accompanying procedures, and you can use these procedures to find the descriptions of the manual entries, thus learning the requirements for the data elements.

Describing dates, social security numbers, telephone numbers, zip codes, or shoe sizes is easy: these data elements have known limits and formats. But other data elements are not so well defined by common usage. Quantities and amounts need to be described as to their limits — how high can they get? can they be negative? how many decimal places? and so on. Data elements that contain nomenclature are usually called names, addresses, descriptions, remarks, and such. Their lengths must be determined. Account numbers, vendor numbers, client numbers, employee numbers, part numbers, stock numbers, customer numbers, and untold numbers of other numbers are not built to any standard whatsoever. Many of them are called numbers but consist of letters and punctuation as well as digits.

The point to emphasize here is that you must clearly define the physical properties of all the data elements that will be in the data base. You must get as much of this definition process done as possible before you proceed with further design. Then you must build the data element dictionary.

A hint: find someone in the user community to approve your data element dictionary. If no one will put a signature to your work at this point in the design, the requirements are not that clearly understood by you or them. More analysis needs to be done before the design proceeds.

GATHER THE DATA ELEMENTS INTO FILES

When you separate the data elements from the aggragates, the aggregates are left over. Those aggregates must be dealt with, and chances are they are going to be files.

Following are the data items that were left out of the data element dictionary:

employees, departments, projects, schedules, and assignments

You can look at your requirements to see which of the above items should be files in your data base. None of the requirements calls for the permanent retention of specific schedule records. The information that might be used to report a schedule condition is information that would be recorded about a project (the dates, the budget) or an assignment (the hours worked). So you can drop schedules from the list, and those that remain are the files.

It now remains for you to describe the files. Remember from Chapter 2 that a file is a collection of records. To define a file, you must define the format of the record that it stores. To define the record, you specify the data elements that will appear in it.

Use your trusty 3×5 cards for this next exercise where you will walk through the procedure for defining the employees file from Chapter 2. Fan out the cards and pull out everything solely related to the category of employee. This is not as simple as it sounds. It is obvious that the department name is not related to the employee and that the employee name is. But is the data element that records the hours worked by an employee on a project specifically related to the employee? It is not, at least not immediately. You cannot put that data element into the employee's record because there could be a number of different values for that element for the same employee — the employee can work on multiple projects. The department name is not related to the employee, but is the department number? Yes. An employee is assigned to a department, and only one department, and the departments are identified by department number. So the department number can be a part of the employee record.

By examining each data element, and viewing it in the light of its relevance to an employee, you can build a stack of 3×5 cards that are the data elements for the employee record. This stack will contain the cards for the employee number, employee name, date hired, salary, and department number. If you refer to the schema used in Chapter 2, you will see that this list corresponds to the EMPLOYEES file description.

You now need to design the rest of the files in the data base. Remember that you are never done. Always be willing to change what you have done before. Do not allow your current design task to be constrained by the ones that preceded it. If you cannot get something designed correctly because of an earlier design, then retreat and review that earlier design.

IDENTIFY THE RETRIEVAL CHARACTERISTICS OF EACH FILE

Once the files are laid out, you need to specify the methods of retrieval that are required by each. You have several alternatives, and a design might consist of any combination of them.

The purpose for identifying the retrieval requirements of the data base is so that you can decide which fields should be primary key index values, which fields should be secondary index values, and which files should be related as discussed in a later section.

Following are the kinds of retrievals that a system could perform.

Specific Key Retrieval

Suppose you work at the computer and call for the display of a selected record. To do this, you need to know something about the data values in the record that is to be retrieved. To retrieve a record from the EMPLOYEES file, a user will know different information depending on who the user is. One user might know the employee number while another knows the employee's name.

A retrieval request is called a **query** and is expressed as search criteria in a query expression. A specific key retrieval will identify the key data element and the data value being searched for. Any record that matches the expressed retrieval criteria will appear in the response. The following is what a condition looks like:

```
dept_no = 123
```

If you use this expression to retrieve records from the EMPLOYEES file, records that have the value 123 in the department number data element will be retrieved.

The retrieval is the expression of the search critria. The response is the record or records that are retrieved when the retrieval is processed.

Some key retrievals will be based on a partial value of a data element. You might know that the employee's last name is Smith. You might not know the precise spelling of the name. In these cases, the retrieval must be able to deliver a response that contains a list of those records that are in the neigborhood of the specified key. Then you can make a more precise selection.

Some key retrievals can deliver only one record. A retrieval against the EMPLOYEES file that uses a specific employee number as the specified key will deliver only the matching employee record (if one exists that matches the specified key value).

Some key retrievals will deliver multiple records. If, for example, you retrieve employee records that contain a specified department number, as was done in the example above, the response will be a list of those employees (if any) who are assigned to the specified department.

You must understand the nature of the response to a given retrieval because you must know whether you can display the record as a full-screen template that contains all of the data in the record or whether a list of retrieved records is to be displayed.

Some retrievals will tell you how many responses occurred. You can then decide whether or not the retrieval responses should be viewed. If you get 49,000 responses from a file of 50,000 records, you are not likely to want to page through all of them.

Key Range Searches

Your retrievals might be based on a range of values for a given data element. For example, you might be required to provide a report of all employees who were hired this month or those who are in a particular salary scale.

Range searches must always be expected to deliver more than one record for each retrieval.

Boolean Query Retrievals

A Boolean query is one that uses the rules of Boolean logic. A series of true/false conditions are combined in an expression that uses three operators: AND, OR, and NOT. The conditions are expressions that match data element values to key values in the retrieval.

Here are two conditions that are combined with a Boolean operator:

```
dept_no = 123 AND salary < 20,000
```

This expression will retrieve records for employees who are assigned to department 123 and whose salaries are less than $20,000.

As with programming languages, Boolean expressions can use parentheses to provide the precedence of the search. Consider these two expressions where the data elements and relational operators are the same but where parentheses define the precedence of the expression:

```
dept_no=123 AND (salary < 20,000 OR date_hired > 01/01/80)

(dept_no=123 AND salary < 20,000) OR date hired > 01/01/80
```

The first expression would retrieve any employee in department 123 who either makes less than $20,000 or who was hired after January 1, 1980.

The second expression would retrieve the record for any employee in department 123 whose salary is less than $20,000 or any employee in any department who was hired after January 1, 1980.

File Scans: Select, Sort, and Display

Many of your retrievals will consist of scanning a file from beginning to end, selecting records that match your search criteria, sorting the selected records into a new sequence, and preparing a response from the selected records in the new sequence. You can distinguish these retrievals from the on-line retrievals by the frequency of the process (how often is it done?), the urgency of need for the response (how soon is it needed?), and the expected number of records in the response (how big is it?).

If a retrieval is done periodically in a routine fashion against a fixed criteria, then the requirement is likely a report rather than an on-line retrieval. The production of a periodic report can be done by the computer when it is not being used for on-line tasks, i.e., when a person is not needed to run it.

It is to your advantage to have as many of the retrieval requirements as posssible fulfilled by reports. Their production does not demand your attention (beyond starting the program), and they do not require the use of key indexes to provide their responses. Key indexes are required for many of your retrievals, but they exact a cost. Each data element in a file that is identified as a key index is supported by another file to store the index, which implies a storage overhead for each index. Whenever a record is added to, changed in, or deleted from a data base file, the supporting index files must be modified accordingly. This requirement implies a processing overhead for each index.

Multiple-File Retrievals

So far, retrievals have been discussed as if they were always performed against individual files. But often you will process retrievals where the responses consist of data elements taken from more than one file in the data base.

If you are required to display the employee number, the employee name, and the department number of the department where the employee is assigned, then you can get all that information from the EMPLOYEES file in the PERSONNEL data base. But if the requirement is to display the department name as well, then you must build your response from data elements taken from two files because the department name is not in the EMPLOYEES file.

To support this search, you must first locate the employee record, which will be based on the search criteria specified in the query expression. Since each employee record has the department number in it, you will use that department number to retrieve the matching department record in the DEPARTMENTS file. The department name from the department record goes into your response.

Using a data element from a record in one file to find a record in another file is the basis for the relational data model. With this technique, you can describe retrieval paths that navigate the many files in the data base, gathering data elements to form a response to a retrieval.

A retrieval that uses data elements from more than one file implies that a relationship exists among the files. This relationship leads into the next discussion of interfile relationships.

IDENTIFY THE RELATIONSHIPS BETWEEN FILES

In a relational data base, files are usually related when they contain common data elements where the data element is the primary key to one of the files. In the PERSONNEL data base, the EMPLOYEES file is related to the DEPARTMENTS file because the employee record includes the department number data element, and the department number is the primary key to the DEPARTMENTS file.

Because of this relationship, you can view the DEPARTMENTS file from two perspectives based on the two purposes it serves. First, it is the system's record of everything related to a department. All by itself, it could be a DEPARTMENTS data base rather than a file in a larger data base. It needs nothing from the EMPLOYEES file to complete its charter. Second, the DEPARTMENTS file is the table of information about the department in which an employee works. It is used to validate the department number when one is being stored in an employee's record and is also used to provide the name of the department for an employee.

This relationship implies some responsibility. For it to be effective, it must have integrity. If an employee record contains a department number, there should be a matching department record. If no such department record exists, the integrity of the data base has been compromised. This condition is caused by one of two circumstances: (1) a program has added a department number to an employee record without first checking the department file; (2) a program has deleted a department record without checking for the existence of its department number in the employee records.

Your applications software is responsible for ensuring the integrity of these relationships. Whenever you add a department number to an employee record, you can retrieve the department record. If it isn't there, the department number you are adding is invalid. If you make the department number a secondary key into the EMPLOYEE file, then you can enforce the relationship in the other direction. Whenever you want to delete a department record, you can do a retrieval to see if any employee records have the department number. If so, the delete should not occur because the integrity of the relationship would be compromised.

There can be other relationships not shown by the appearance of key data elements in files. These relationships are defined by your retrieval requirements. You might not have realized that you needed to record a key data element in a file when you designed that file. Look at the output requirements to see if you missed any relationships, and change your file design where appropriate.

You must evaluate each such potential relationship to see if it is real. In some cases, a controlling number is recorded in a record as information only. Users do not care if its corresponding record is still in the other file; it may have been retired.

More often, the relationships are real and must be protected. In one-to-one and one-to-many relationships, the software must preserve data integrity. In the case of the many-to-many relationship, you must provide a connector file to support the relationship, and then you must ensure that it is always synchronized with the two files it connects.

The relationships between files can describe potential retrieval paths for multiple-file retrievals. Sometimes, the apparent paths are incorrect. Figure 3.1 shows the PERSONNEL data base and the relationships between the three files. If you designed a retrieval that began by retrieving a department record, each project for the department, and then each employee who is assigned to each project, you might not have the answer you are looking for. If the purpose of the retrieval is to list the employees who are working on projects that are assigned to the department, then the response is correct. But if the retrieval is supposed to deliver a list of employees who work in the department, then the response is incorrect. In this case, you have chosen a retrieval path based on interfile dependencies that don't work. Remember from the requirements that an employee in one department can work on a project that is assigned to a different department. The data base design supports these relationships, but, as seen in this example, the potential exists for you to describe paths that deliver incorrect results. This is not a flaw in the data base design. It is correct. The problem lies in the description of a retrieval path. You must develop these paths carefully to ensure that the answer is going to be the one you are looking for.

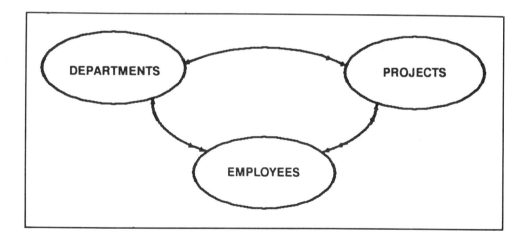

Figure 3.1   Retrieval Paths

DEVELOP THE SCHEMA FOR THE DBMS YOU ARE USING

This last step requires knowledge of the schema language of the data base management system that you will be using. You must translate the pile of 3×5 cards and diagrams into a format that the DBMS can understand. The next chapter provides more detail on the nature of the DBMS and its schema language.

SUMMARY

Now you have an idea of what constitutes a data base and how to design one. So where can you go from here? A data base design is of little use without a software system to process it. Data base software comes in two parts—your applications programs that process the data records in their functional formats and the general-purpose system of software that manages data base definition, organization, storage, and retrieval. This software is called the **data base management system** or **DBMS**, which the next chapter describes.

CHAPTER 4

THE DATA BASE
MANAGEMENT SYSTEM

Chapters 2 and 3 discussed the data base, its architecture, and its design. This chapter covers the data base management system, which is the software used to manage data base descriptions, data storage, and data retrieval in data base applications. When you develop software for an application, you do not want to reinvent wheels. Why develop code to read and write records, maintain index files, and store and retrieve data? These processes have common requirements in most systems. You shouldn't need to rewrite them every time you build a new application.

THE DBMS

Packaged software exists that manages routine storage and retrieval of data in data bases. This software is called the **data base management system** or **DBMS**. The DBMS sits between the application programs and the data base and stores and retrieves data records. It runs with and responds to requests from the application software. Figure 4.1 shows the relationship between the application programs, the DBMS, and the data base.

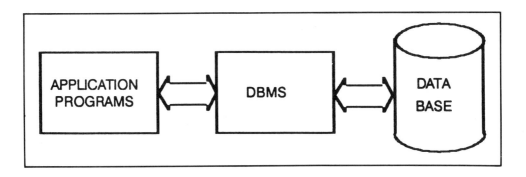

Figure 4.1   Managing the Data Base

When an application program needs a record from the data base, it calls the DBMS and passes it parameters that tell the DBMS how to retrieve the record. This call can be a request such as "find the inventory record with stock number 0123." The DBMS finds the record and passes a copy of it back to the application program. When the application program has a record to write to the data base, it calls the DBMS and passes a copy of the record. The DBMS places the record in an appropriate location where applications programs can later find it. Any indexing of the record and any relationships it has with other records in other files in the data base are managed and maintained by the DBMS. All the applications programs need to know is that they have originated or retrieved a record, changed it, and returned it to the data base.

COMMERCIAL DBMS PACKAGES

To use a data base, you must have access to one, usually through a DBMS. If you work with a mainframe or minicomputer, you might develop software with a large commercial DBMS. If you develop software for the IBM PC, you might use one of the DBMS packages available in that environment. Most packages will support a large, complex data base. Some spreadsheet programs offer a data base manager function. Spreadsheet data bases are usually limited to fit within the capacity of the spreadsheet as determined by the software and the memory available on your machine.

You can apply the ideas discussed in Chapter 2 to commercially available data base packages. These packages have their advantages and weaknesses. If you use any of these packages to develop medium and large data base systems, you will find they have mixed blessings and curses. They all share two disadvantages — the cost per copy for use is high, and the tendency for their developers to release improved versions that make older versions obsolete is frequent. Cost can be important. When you develop software to sell, you want to be able to install it in as many different sites as possible. It must be attractively and competitively priced. You might even want to give the software away as an incentive or a promotion. Suppose you develop a system to support a large potential customer base. To sell the system, you must provide the supporting software required to run it, which includes the DBMS. If it is necessary to add several hundred dollars to the sale price to cover the cost of a DBMS license, you might not be competitive, or the price might not be as attractive as it could be.

Consider another problem with packages. A recent project involved the development of a software system that was installed in several locations. The system included a word processor, a DBMS, and custom software for the IBM PC. Development of the custom software was under way for about a year. On the basis of some benchmarks, the word processor and DBMS packages were selected because of their features and their performance. Once the project was under steam with a commitment to these packages, the vendors decided to improve them. The improvements were a disaster for the project; the custom software no longer worked with the text file produced by the word processor, and the DBMS itself no longer worked as it once did.

You can't fault the word processing people for making their product better; they want to maintain their competitive position; however, you can fault the DBMS vendor for releasing a new, improved, bug-ridden product. Both new packages (the one that worked and the one that did not) took their toll on the project. Because the project team was not in control of the development of the packages, it could not influence impact of those packages on the requirements of the project. The obvious solution was to retreat to the earlier versions, but earlier versions were no longer supported and licenses were not available to use them.

DBMS packages can restrict use with limits and boundaries. A data base can have no more than a specified number of files; a file can have only so many records; a record can have a limited number of data elements and only so many characters; the number of key data elements might be limited. The list of limitations has no limit. One nationally advertised DBMS reduced the number of data elements allowed in a file in a new (improved) version; however, the company forgot to improve their advertising and documentation to communicate this improvement. Another brand-name DBMS imposes a limit of 128 data elements per file. This restriction is justified by the claim that a data base with more than 128 data elements is unwieldy.

Such a system would encounter harsh realities if it tried to automate something for a large bureaucracy where fiefdoms survive and are protected. There is a control number for everything, a code for everything, an acronym for everything, an organization in charge of everything, and a date when everything happened. Users won't part with any of the data elements and want everything in one file so they can write queries without understanding data base architecture. It is nearly impossible to fit all the information into 128 data elements.

You should understand why DBMS packages have limits. The software needs maximum values for its array dimensions and its buffer sizes, but you, the programmer, are stuck with whatever the DBMS developer decides are reasonable limits. You cannot increase the limits, even if you have a lot of memory in your computer, and you cannot trade one limit for another to suit a particular application problem because you do not have the source code to the DBMS.

Many DBMS packages have yet another disadvantage. The formats of data files and indexes are hidden from the software developer. If you need to develop a utility function for data management, a lack of knowledge of the data base internal structures can hamper your efforts. The same circumstance prevents you from integrating the data base with other software systems that do not use the DBMS. A system that does not reveal its internals to its users has a **closed** architecture. In almost every case, a closed architecture is advantageous to those who sell the system and a hindrance to those who try to use it.

AN ALTERNATIVE TO THE DBMS PACKAGE

There are alternatives to using a package. The C programmer will find few DBMS products with functions that a C program can call. Until recently, most IBM PC DBMS packages provided their own application language and did not support calls from other programming languages. To accomodate today's trends, some of the vendors offer a C developer's toolkit; however, most such kits produce code that fares poorly when compared with the efficiency of the typical C program. This book presents alternatives to using a DBMS, which involves a library of C functions that do for you what a DBMS would do. The advantages to this approach are the efficiency of the resulting system, the absence of licensing costs, the control you have over the DBMS and its destiny, and the open architecture of the data base files and indexes.

DATA BASE MANAGEMENT SYSTEM FUNDAMENTALS

If you are to build your own DBMS, you should understand the fundamentals of DBMS technology. These fundamentals will define the basis for the software system that you build in the following chapters.

A DBMS is used to manage a data base. You express the data base design in a format that the DBMS can interpret. On one side are applications programs wanting to get at the data records; on the other side is the data base on disk waiting to be processed. In the middle is the DBMS, which passes data back and forth between the programs and the data base. For the DBMS to pass this information, something must tell it what the data in the data base look like. Statements called the **Data Definition Language** provide a description of the data base in a format that the DBMS can interpret. Once the DBMS knows the format and organization of the data, it must have a way to communicate with the application programs. An interprogram protocol called the **Data Manipulation Language** provides this communication. To build a DBMS, you must consider how these two languages will look.

The Data Definition Language

In Chapter 2, a small personnel data base was designed by describing the data elements, the files, and the relationships between the files. The design took the form of tables that listed the characteristics of each data element and each file. Those tables are a statement of the format of the data base, and, as such, constitute a Data Definition Language; however, to be useful in a DBMS, the tables must be in a format that the computer can translate into physical storage characteristics for the data. After you design the data base, write the DDL. It is a language just as C is a language. And just as there are many programming languages, there are many DDLs. Which DDL you use depends on which DBMS you use. So, even if you design the data base with tables such as those shown in Chapter 2, you must still express that design in a DDL suitable to your DBMS. Figure 4.2 shows the data base design reduced to a DDL that the DBMS can read.

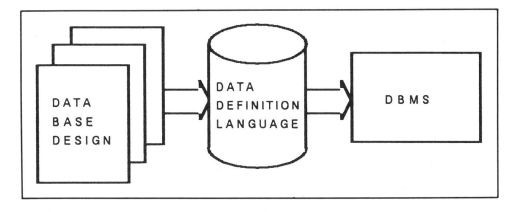

Figure 4.2   The Data Definition Language

Various techniques exist for writing the DDL. One widely used technique is to write the DDL statements into a text file much as you would build the source file for a program. Some DBMS packages use a DDL compiler program to process the DDL file into tables the DBMS can understand. Others have the DBMS interpret the DDL in its original code. In this book, C language statements will be used to express the DDL. Chapter 6 discusses the characteristics of the C language that make this expression possible. Later, you will use a DDL compiler program that translates a text DDL into the C language DDL.

Data Models

When designing a DDL, you must be aware of the data model that the DBMS supports. Data base terminology defines the data model as one of three traditional forms for the organization of data: the hierarchical model, the network model, and the relational model.

A **hierarchical** data base is one where the relationships between the files form a hierarchy. In a hierarchy, files rank from top to bottom, with higher level files being the parents of lower files. Figure 4.3 shows a hierarchy of a department's employees and projects. In a hierarchy, a file may have several child files, but each child file may have only one parent file.

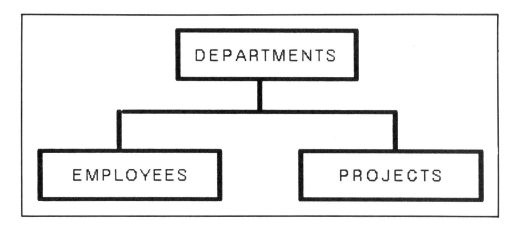

Figure 4.3   The Hierarchical Data Model

A **network** data base is similar to a hierarchical data base except that a file can have multiple parents. In Figure 4.4, the organization of the three files shows that the project file is a parent of the employee file.

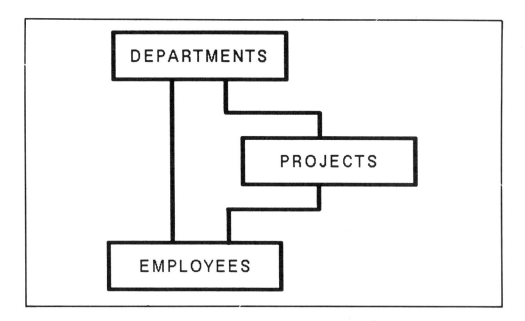

Figure 4.4   The Network Data Model

In the **relational** data base, files have no parents and no children. They are unrelated. Figure 4.5 shows the three files in a relational data base.

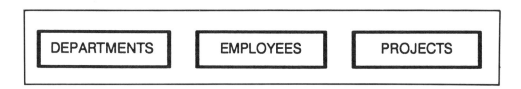

Figure 4.5   The Relational Data Model

These models don't seem to make any sense. The files are the same in all three models, but the lines connecting them are different, and the relational model is the one where the files are unrelated.

The lines between the files define the physical relationships that the DBMS establishes and maintains. The lines represent internal pointers that are recorded in the records and that point to the records hosted by the parents. Data bases supported by hierarchical and network DBMSs contain control values inside the records to establish the relationships. These values are pointers unseen by the user and maintained by the DBMS. In Figures 4.3 and 4.4, the departments are connected to the employees. Several techniques exist for this connection, and the one used will depend on the DBMS. In one method, the record address of the department record is stored in the employee record. Another technique involves the department record pointing to the first of several employee records. The employee records then each point to the next record in a chain of those belonging to the department.

What about the relational model? If the files are unrelated, how do you know what employee works in what department? Relate files by using data elements. The department number is included as a data element in the employee file. It is a relational data model because the data forms the relationships. The discussions in Chapter 2 are built upon the relational data model, and the DBMS that will be developed in later chapters is a relational DBMS.

The relational model has advantages and weaknesses. The major advantage is that it is the easiest model to build a DBMS for, which is why it is so popular among DBMS vendors.

The relational model has two drawbacks, however. First, the model it-self does not enforce relationships. In a situation such as the one in Figure 4.5, you can have an employee who has no department. Worse, you can assign an employee to a department that does not exist. The model does not prevent this situation from happening. In the relational data model, the integrity of interfile relationships is the responsibility of applications programs. They must determine that the department record exists before they add or change an employee record. To delete a department record, the application programs must ensure that the department has no employees assigned to it. In the hierarchical and net-work models, the DBMS usually enforces these relationships because the pointers must be there and they must point to valid records. In the relational model, enforcement of data integrity is the responsibility of the programmer.

The second drawback to the relational model occurs when two files in the data base have a many-to-many relationship. Suppose that employees can work on several projects, and each project can use several employees, as in Figure 2.6. For a hierarchical or network data base, the DBMS maintains a pointer mechanism invisible to the user and programmer. For the relational model, the data base designer designs a connector file into the data base. In Chapter 2, the connector file was referred to as the ASSIGNMENTS file. Such a file often exists only to support the relationship. It is a contrived structure because of the nature of the model, and, usually, the programmer and the user must be aware of it.

Nonetheless, the relational data base is the backbone of most DBMS packages for the IBM PC and is the approach taken for this book's al-ternative DBMS; however, you must recognize the need to enforce relationships. Chapter 6 will explain how, if you design your data base properly, the DBMS will not allow you to assign employees to nonex-istent departments.

The world is a network. The things and people in it tend to have com-plex, many-to-many relationships with one another. If you have ever designed a data base for a system to support what was previously a manual application, you know that people will build complex and con-voluted systems for themselves. They find comfort and security in the understanding and operation of esoteric mechanisms.

A requirements analysis was once conducted to develop the initial design for a data base. The automated system was to track the status of engineering documentation. The user had an existing manual system consisting of many forms, drawings, and documents. To derive their relationships, a questionnaire was designed to determine, for all combinations of document pairs, if the relationships were one-to-one, one-to-many, or many-to-many. The questions were in the form of true-false statements such as "There may be many Engineering Orders for a given Drawing; True or False." An analyst interviewed the proprietors of these documents to determine the relationships. Amazingly, every relationship in every pair from a dozen documents was many-to-many.

The reduction of such a mess into a relational data model involves a multi-step process called **normalization**. Several books explain this procedure in detail. Two excellent examples are listed here:

James Martin, *Computer Data-Base Organization*, Second Edition, Prentice-Hall, Inc., 1977.

C.J. Date, *An Introduction to Database Systems*, Second Edition, Addison-Wesley Publishing Company, 1977.

It is not within the scope of this book to tackle the weighty subject of normalization. It is recommended that you read either of the two references just cited; they both cover the subject of data base technology and are valuable to anyone involved in data base design and programming.

Incidentally, computer science writers do not agree on how the term "data base" should be written. Martin hyphenates the term ("data-base"). Date makes it one word ("database"). Others, including the author of this book, have chosen not to extend the English language but to use the two existing words ("data base").

The Data Manipulation Language

Given a Data Definition Language (DDL) to describe the data base to the DBMS, you need a corresponding language for programs to use so they can communicate with the DBMS. Such a language is called the Data Manipulation Language (DML), and it and part of the DDL are used whenever an application program wants access to the data. The DDL describes the records to the application program, and the DML provides an interface to the DBMS. The first uses record formats, and the second uses external function calls, both in the fashion of the host programming language. The record formats are a part of the DDL that translates data definition into data manipulation. To retrieve and update records, you must know their formats. The calls to functions provide ways to store and retrieve data to and from the data base. Figure 4.6 shows how the DDL relates the DBMS and the application programs and how the DDL and the DML provide communication between the DBMS and the programs.

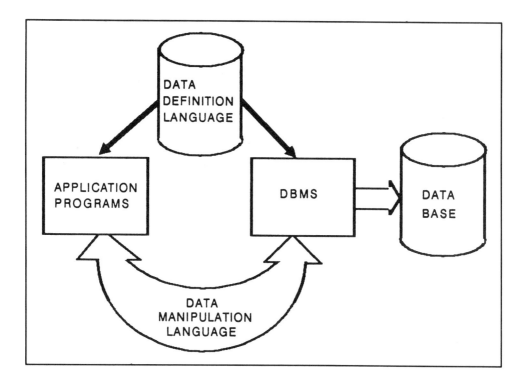

Figure 4.6   The Data Manipulation Language

The DML must provide functional access to the data base. This access includes functions that retrieve records from files by key search, add records to files, delete records from files, retrieve records sequentially in a key sequence, retrieve records in the physical sequence in which they are recorded, and rewrite records that have been updated.

DBMS Utility Programs

Most DBMS software packages will include more than a DDL and a DML. To support the management of data in a data base and to allow infrequent ad hoc retrievals of the data, the DBMS usually has a library of utility programs including a data entry program, a query package, a sort, and a report writer. Other useful utilities for tending the data base are index-building tools, a program to initialize the data base files with null data, and programs to convert files when you modify the schema.

A general-purpose data entry program allows you to specify a file and a subset of its data elements and then to add, change, or delete records in the file using a screen displaying the data elements.

A DBMS query utility program allows you to extract data from the data base by specifying a file name, a list of data elements to extract from the file, and a set of select criteria. The select criteria are usually in an expression involving some data elements in the file and some constants in the expression. The program tests each record against the criteria, and if the expression returns a true value, it selects the record. Selected records can be sent to the screen, the printer, or to a new file for processing. In some DBMS packages, the new file can become part of the data base.

A sort utility changes the sequence of a file that is usually selected by a query.

A report writer utility program reads a data base file or a file selected by a query program and builds a report from it.

Index builders rebuild index files, which can correct an index that has been contaminated, perhaps as the result of a power failure.

The program that initializes the data base creates the data and index files and initializes them with null data.

You need conversion programs when you modify the data base schema after the data base has been in use. A conversion program must know about the old schema and the new one. It reads file records using the old schema and writes them using the new schema. New data elements are set to null values.

A DBMS will include most of these utility functions in one form or another. The extent and complexity of the support provided by a particular utility program depends on the package itself.

SUMMARY

Chapters 2 through 4 have established the groundwork for the approach to an automated data base. The next chapter begins to reveal the technique for having data base management software without having a commercial data base management system. You can build your schema in source code such that applications programs are unaware of the properties of the data and its indexes, and the DBMS is unaware of the specifics of the application that the DBMS supports. This code requires a programming language with certain language constructs that support these goals. C is such a language, as you will see in Chapter 5.

CHAPTER 5

C AS A
DATA DEFINITION LANGUAGE

Chapters 2 and 3 discussed data bases and design; Chapter 4 discussed the Data Base Management System. Following this chapter, Chapter 6 presents a DBMS that is available to the C programmer in the IBM PC environment. The technique involved uses features of the C language to emulate the Data Definition and Data Manipulation Languages of larger, more complex systems. These languages include three components of the automated data base environment:

- the schema
- the applications software
- the DBMS

First, you describe the schema in a source code module that you include in the applications source program and compile into a relocatable object module. Then you link this module with the DBMS. You compile the DBMS separately with external references to a generic schema. When you link the applications program to the DBMS, the references to a nonspecific schema in the DBMS are resolved with the schema source program. With this approach, the schema and the DBMS become a part of the applications program in one executable object program. Figure 5.1 illustrates this technique.

This approach is a departure from the traditional DBMS environment where you record the schema as a set of schematic tables, usually in special schema disk files. In that environment, the DBMS runs in the computer as a resident task, sometimes called a **kernel**, ready to accept and execute data base requests from transient applications programs. More than one program can actively access the DBMS at one time, and more than one data base can be involved.

In the IBM PC, programs execute in a single-user, single-task environment. It can be assumed that a DBMS kernel and an off-line schema description are unnecessary. Each program in this approach is self-contained; together, they include everything needed to manage the data base. The schema is a set of external arrays; the DBMS is a library of reusable C functions, and each application's function individually supports its specific purpose. You link all three together into a single executable code module as shown in Figure 5.1. To support this technique, the programming language requires certain features. You will find these features in C.

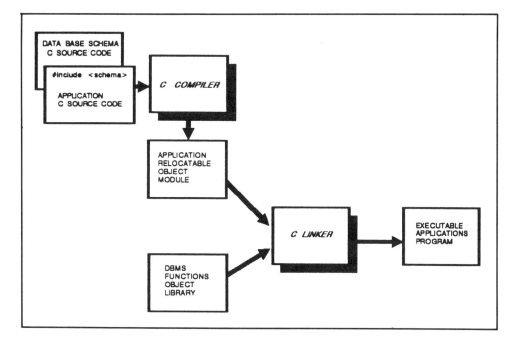

Figure 5.1   Building a Cdata Application

The programming language must allow the assignment of global alphanumeric names to integral values. To describe a data base schema that adjusts itself to modifications in the data formats, you must be able to give names to files and data elements. As the number of names grows or diminishes, the software should adjust without attention. The files will be called by their names, and the software will use the names to offset into tables of data elements. The data elements will also be called by name, and the software will use those names to offset into tables of types and lengths. Remember from Chapters 2 and 3 that you describe a data base by a file list, and you describe a file by a data element list. You want these to be lists of integers. They could be ASCII string lists, but that would involve the memory overhead of string storage and the execution overhead of string searches. In almost every case, the DBMS must reduce the names to integers for subscripts into the schema tables. Integer lists are used here because they are easier and faster to process.

C includes the **#define** preprocessor macro. You can use it to equate the file names and data element names to integers. Consider this list of file names:

```
#define PROJECTS 0
#define EMPLOYEES 1
#define DEPARTMENTS 2
```

Consider this list of data elements:

```
#define EMPLOYEE_NO 1
#define EMPLOYEE_NAME 2
#define DATE_HIRED 3
```

By using the **#define** preprocessor macro, you assign integers to the names of the files and data elements. Now you can build integer arrays that contain instances of these names in a way that is readable to both programmer and machine. The source language has data elements and file names that have meaning, and the software has integers to process. You can seem to pass file names and data element names to functions that are expecting integral values. The library functions that store and retrieve data base records can use these values as subscripts into the tables of the schema.

The next requirement is for the programming language to support multiple source files that are independently compiled. (Some dialects of Pascal and BASIC are deficient in this respect.) The DBMS is code in a source file, and you do not want to compile it every time you compile an applications program. The DBMS should be available as a relocatable object module. You should not have to recompile it every time you change the application. The C language supports this requirement for independently compiled source modules.

The language must also support variable identifiers that are significant to enough positions to allow their use as file and data element names. The significance should provide for names long enough to be titles on reports and queries because that is how you will use them. Originally, the C language supported identifiers significant to the first eight positions. This length is too short for your purposes here. Recent improvements to the language have extended the significance of identifiers to 31 positions for names within a source file, which works in this case. You do not need long names across source files because each of your applications source files will include the **#define** preprocessor macros, and the library functions deal only with the integer equivalents of the file and data element names.

Early C compilers did not allow the members of structures to share the same name unless the members occupied the same relative position within the structures and were of the same type. More recent improvements to the language have removed this restriction, and most compilers have adopted the new rules. The approach used here requires this improvement.

The language must also support external variable types and should not be a "strongly typed" language. To understand this concept, consider what "strongly typed" means.

A strongly typed language is one that at run time enforces the types and dimensions of variables. If a function expects a certain type of variable as a parameter (for example, an integer), then any violation of this type by a calling function is seen as an error when the function is executed. Further, if an array is of a certain size (dimension), then any attempt to subscript an element outside of the array's bounds is an error. These rules constitute strong typing, and will not work here.

In C, a function can pass the address of a structure to another function; the called function can be expecting the address of something else, and the called function can work correctly. This feature is made use of here.

C allows a function to declare an external array with specified dimensions. A separately compiled module can operate on that array without knowing its dimensions. Here is an example:

```
/* source file A */
int i [] = {1,2,3,4,0};
main()
{
    foo();
}

/* source file B */
extern int i[];
foo()
{
    int *j = i;
    while (*j)
    printf("\n%d", *j++);
}
```

Integer array **i** in source file A contains five elements. In source file B, it is known only as an array of integers. The assumption is that the code that uses the integer array will somehow determine its length. In the example, the terminating zero value defines the end of the table. The critical feature is the ability of the function named **foo** to subscript beyond the known boundaries of an array. If you change source file A so that the array is a different length, you do not need to recompile source file B or attend to it in any way. All you must do is relink B's object module with A after A has been recompiled.

In a variation on this feature, the array is a local variable inside the **main** function. **Main** passes the address of the array to the **foo** function, which accepts it as an integer pointer rather than as an array of integers. Once again, the **foo** function is unaware of the dimensions of the array. It only cares that the integer list is terminated with a zero value integer.

```
main()
{
    static int i [] = {1,2,3,4,0};
    foo(i);
}

foo(j)
int *j;
{
    while (*j)
    printf("\n%d", *j++);
}
```

These advantages of the C language are significant in a systems programming environment. Their implications are extensive, and you rely on them to support a data definition language. Since you will define a file name as an integer and records as lists of data element integers, you can allow the following.

The DBMS functions that manipulate records can, given a file name (integer), subscript to an array of data elements (integers) without knowing the length of the array, which means you can compile the DBMS functions once, and then link them with many different applications and many different schemas for many different data bases without having to modify the DBMS code.

There is one final requirement for a programming language that will support this approach to a data base schema. The language must have a rich set of data pointer operations. This area is one in which C shines. C contains facilities for pointers to arrays and structures, pointers to pointers, pointers to arrays of pointers, and so on, as well as a close association between pointers and arrays. C has a rich set of pointer operations, all of which are critical to this approach to a data definition language. These features are also the most difficult aspects of the C language to master. Probably no one has become totally comfortable with some of the ways you can write code for pointer and array operations in C. After several years of C programming, a programmer still needs to shift some mental gears in order to understand what happens to a pointer to a multiply-dimensioned array of pointers to an array of structure member arrays of function pointers. It is fortunate that this situation doesn't happen often.

CHAPTER 6

CDATA: THE CHEAP DATA BASE MANAGEMENT SYSTEM

As explained in Chapter 5, the facilities of the C language can be used to describe the schema of an integrated data base in the relational data model. This technique and the C functions that support it are called **Cdata**, the Cheap Data Base Management System. Cdata is not a product name; it is an abbreviation used in this book to identify the technique.

To describe the approach, a consultant's billing system has been designed. This system is a no-frills application that exists primarily to illustrate the data base software; however, it is functional, and a consulting firm could use it. This system allows a consulting firm to track labor charges and expenses against clients' projects and to prepare invoices.

The Consultant's Billing System (**CBS**) has a data base that records time and expense charges against projects for clients. It prepares invoices for labor hours and expenses, and it computes labor charges from the hourly rates of consultants assigned to projects. You can post expenses directly.

The above paragraphs describe the problem definition for the system — the initial stage in data base design as discussed in Chapter 3.

This new data base is not the PERSONNEL data base used in the examples in the previous chapters. Although the two are similar, there are several differences. The intial design processes described in Chapter 3 will not be restated here. Instead, assume that the nine steps of data base design have been completed and that you have a workable design for the CBS data base. The data base will have four files: a CONSULTANTS file, a CLIENTS file, a PROJECTS file, and an ASSIGNMENTS file. The rest of the design is revealed as it is translated into the Cdata schema.

In Chapter 8, you will build a software system around the CBS data base to show how you integrate applications code with the Cdata Data Manipulation Language.

THE CDATA DATA DEFINITION LANGUAGE

Cdata uses a DDL similar to the approach discussed in earlier chapters. In its first incarnation, the Cdata DDL was built by using C language statements that were compiled along with the applications programs. This was a workable approach, but maintenance of the DDL was difficult with a complex data base. For that reason, the Cdata schema compiler program was developed to make the task simpler. Before the compiler is discussed, DDL C language statements that you compile along with your application will be covered. Then you will see how the compiler can serve as the shortcut for preparing and maintaining the DDL.

The Cdata Data Element Dictionary

One step in the design of the CBS data base is the development of a data element dictionary. By using the approach from Chapters 2 and 3, you can build this table of data elements:

Data Element Name	Data Type	Length
client__no	numeric	5
client__name	alphanumeric	25
address	alphanumeric	25
city	alphanumeric	25
state	alphanumeric	2
zip	numeric	5
phone	numeric	10
amt__due	currency	8
project__no	numeric	5
project__name	alphanumeric	25
amt__expended	currency	9
consultant__no	numeric	5
consultant__name	alphanumeric	25
rate	currency	5
payment	currency	9
expense	currency	9
hours	numeric	2
date__paid	date	6

Next, these data elements are described in a format that the applications programs, the DBMS, and the utility programs can use. The characteristics of the dictionary will be expressed in the syntax of the C language.

The first part of the dictionary is a table of definitions that gives mnemonic names to the data elements and equates them to integers. Applications programs will use these global symbols to name the data elements in tables and function parameters. The programs use the schema to assign data elements to files and indexes. Listing 6.1 is the first component of the Cdata data element dictionary and schema for the CBS.

Observe in Listing 6.1 that each data element name from the initial paper design is now a globally defined symbol available to any program that includes the **#define** statements when it is compiled.

Listing 6.1

```
/*
 *  Listing 6-1. Data Element Dictionary Definitions
 */

#define CLIENT_NO 1
#define CLIENT_NAME 2
#define ADDRESS 3
#define CITY 4
#define STATE 5
#define ZIP 6
#define PHONE 7
#define AMT_DUE 8
#define PROJECT_NO 9
#define PROJECT_NAME 10
#define AMT_EXPENDED 11
#define CONSULTANT_NO 12
#define CONSULTANT_NAME 13
#define RATE 14
#define PAYMENT 15
#define EXPENSE 16
#define HOURS 17
```

The Cdata functions need to know the lengths of each of the data elements. An array of integers contains these lengths. Each integer is the length of a data element, and the integer's position in the array tells which data element it belongs to. The first length is for the first data element in Listing 6.1; the second is for the second, and so on. Listing 6.2 shows the array that contains the data element lengths. Each applications program includes it as an external array so that the Cdata functions can derive the data element lengths.

Listing 6.2

```
/*
 *  Listing 6-2.  Data Element Lengths
 */

int ellen [] = {
    5,25,25,25,2,5,10,8,5,25,9,5,25,5,9,9,2
};
```

Some utility programs and functions use string versions of the data element names. The utilities use the strings to display the data element names in queries and reports. They also use the strings to convert data element names entered by the user into integers that the Cdata functions can interpret. Listing 6.3 is the array of character pointers that supply those strings. You compile it with the applications programs and utilities. To work properly with the utility programs that are described in the next chapter, the data element string names must be in uppercase.

Listing 6.3

```
/*
 * Listing 6-3.   Data Element Name Strings
 */

char *denames [] = {
    "CLIENT_NO",
    "CLIENT_NAME",
    "ADDRESS",
    "CITY",
    "STATE",
    "ZIP",
    "PHONE",
    "AMT_DUE",
    "PROJECT_NO",
    "PROJECT_NAME",
    "AMT_EXPENDED",
    "CONSULTANT_NO",
    "CONSULTANT_NAME",
    "RATE",
    "PAYMENT",
    "EXPENSE",
    "HOURS",
    (char *) 0
};
```

The same utility functions that display data element names need the attributes of the data element. These attributes describe the format and content of each data element. By using these attributes, the software knows how to control the data entry and display of the data elements. The utility functions use screen management functions that describe data elements in terms of a display mask and a data element type code. The display mask uses the underscore character to define character positions and allows punctuation characters to appear in the mask. The data element type code is as follows:

A = alphanumeric
C = currency
Z = numeric, zero-filled
N = numeric, space-filled
D = date

Listing 6.4 shows the character array of data element type codes and the array of display mask character pointers that correspond with the CBS data element dictionary. You compile these arrays with the applications programs and utilities as external arrays.

Listing 6.4

```
/*
 * Listing 6-4. Data Element Display Characteristics
 */

char eltype [] = "ZAAAANNCZACZACCCN";
char *elmask [] = {
    "_____",
    "_____",
    "_____.",
    "_____",
    "_____",
    "___",
    "_____",
    "(___)___-____",
    "$_____.__",
    "_____",
    "_____",
    "$_____.__",
    "_____",
    "_____",
    "$___.__",
    "$_____.__",
    "$_____.__",
    "__"
};
```

File Specifications

Next, you need to decide what data files will be in the CBS data base. Since the data base must maintain a record of clients, projects, and consultants, it follows that you will build a data file for each. Figure 6.1 shows the three files and their relationships. The symbolic approach discussed in Chapter 2 is used to illustrate the files.

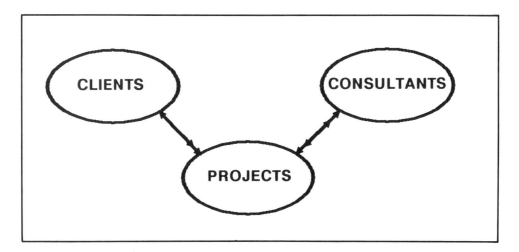

Figure 6.1   The Consultant's Billing System Data Base

A many-to-many relationship exists between consultants and projects, so you must add a connector file to maintain the relationship. Since the connector file stores data about consultants assigned to projects, it is called the ASSIGNMENTS file. Figure 6.2 shows the data base with this file added.

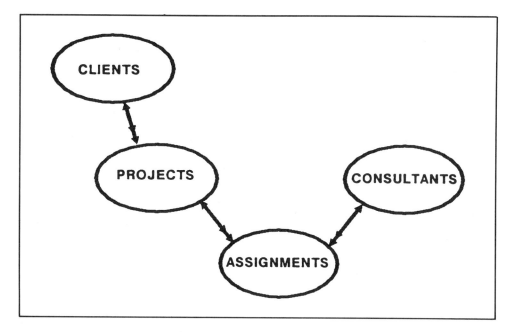

Figure 6.2   Addition of the ASSIGNMENTS File

Next, assign data elements to files by using the approach described in Chapter 2. This effort produces the following table:

CBS:
CLIENTS: client__no, client__name, address, city,
                     state, phone, amt__due, date__paid
PROJECTS: project__no, project__name, amt__expended,
                     client__no
CONSULTANTS: consultant__no, consultant__name
ASSIGNMENTS: consultant__no, project__no, rate

This table is the result of the data base design. Now, you must translate it into the Cdata Data Definition Language.

The expression of the file specifications in the DDL involves three stages. First, tell Cdata the names of the files; next, specify the data elements that are in each file; and, finally, describe record structures for the files.

The first step involves two constructs both seen in Listing 6.5. Just as data elements are equated to integers, so will files be equated to integers. These global definitions are compiled with the programs so that they may use integer values to represent files. Then an array of character pointers to strings is provided that contains the file names. Cdata uses these pointers to build file names so that it can open the data and index files. The utility programs use the file name character pointers to translate user-entered file names into the integers that Cdata expects. For the utility programs to work, the file name strings must be in uppercase letters.

Listing 6.5

```
/*
 *   Listing 6-5. File Specifications
 */

#define CLIENTS 0
#define PROJECTS 1
#define CONSULTANTS 2
#define ASSIGNMENTS 3

char *dbfiles [] = {
    "CLIENTS",
    "PROJECTS",
    "CONSULTANTS",
    "ASSIGNMENTS",
    (char *) 0
};
```

The next step in file specification defines the contents of each file in terms of its data elements. First, an integer array is provided for each file. The array contains an integer for each data element in the file. The integer values come from the global data element definitions of the data element dictionary. Each array is a list of data element integers terminated by a zero value integer. Listing 6.6 shows the four arrays for the CBS data base.

Listing 6.6

```
/*
 * Listing 6-6. File Contents
 */

int clients_file [] = {CLIENT_NO, CLIENT_NAME, ADDRESS,
                       CITY, STATE, ZIP, PHONE, AMT_DUE, 0};
int projects_file [] = {PROJECT_NO, PROJECT_NAME,
                        AMT_EXPENDED, CLIENT_NO, 0};
int consultants_file [] = {CONSULTANT_NO,
                           CONSULTANT_NAME, 0};
int assignments_file [] = {CONSULTANT_NO, PROJECT_NO,
                           RATE, 0};

int *file_ele [] = {
    clients_file,
    projects_file,
    consultants_file,
    assignments_file,
    (int *) 0
};
```

Listing 6.6 also shows a fifth array named **file__ele**, which is an array of
integer pointers. One pointer exists for each file in the data base and
points to the array of data elements for the file. This pointer array allows a program to get the address of a file's description by using this expression:

```
file_ele [filename]
```

The last step in file specification results in a record structure definition
for each file. In this step, you provide a structure that programs can
use to describe a record buffer. The programs read into and write from
the record buffers. The structure's members correspond to the record's
data elements. Their lengths are taken from the data element dictionary with one added for the null string terminator. Listing 6.7 shows the
four structures for the four files in the CBS data base.

Listing 6.7

```
/*
 *  Listing 6-7.  File Record Structures
 */

struct clients {
    char client_no [6];
    char client_name [26];
    char address [26];
    char city [26];
    char state [3];
    char zip [6];
    char phone [11];
    char amt_due [9];
};

struct projects {
    char project_no [6];
    char project_name [26];
    char amt_expended [10];
    char client_no [6];
};

struct consultants {
    char consultant_no [6];
    char consultant_name [26];
};

struct assignments {
    char consultant_no [6];
    char project_no [6];
    char rate [6];
};
```

You will see a convention for data identifier names in the Cdata DDL. Look at the clients file. Its global integer is equated to CLIENTS. Its file description is an array named **clients__file**. Its structure type is named **clients**. Similarly, the members in a structure definition carry the same names as the data elements they represent, except that the global data names are in uppercase while the member names are not. The data element for client number is named **CLIENT__NO**, and its corresponding member name in a record is named **client__no**. If you define a structure of type **clients** with the name **client,** the client number's identifier is **client.client__no**.

Index Specifications

The last part of the DDL tells Cdata which data elements are key indexes in which files. In the example of CBS, the CLIENTS file has the **client__no** as the primary key; the PROJECTS file uses **proj__no**, and the CONSULTANTS file uses **consultant__no**. The ASSIGNMENTS file uses the concatenated data elements **consultant__no** and **project__no**. The data base design is completed with the following table:

CBS:
CLIENTS:	<u>client no</u>, client__name, address, city, state, phone, amt__due, date__paid
PROJECTS:	<u>project no</u>, project__name, amt__expended, client__no
CONSULTANTS:	<u>consultant no</u>, consultant__name
ASSIGNMENTS:	<u>consultant no, project no</u>, rate

The Cdata DDL technique for defining index data elements involves building a series of integer arrays to describe the various key indexes and their characteristics. First, a file can have several different indexes. Second, an index can consist of several concatenated data elements. Both of these dimensions are variable in length, so you must build an array architecture to represent any possibility.

Each index is represented in an integer array that contains the integers for the key data elements. Each key is an array. If a key contains several concatenated data elements, its array contains several data element integers. If a file has several indexes, it will have several arrays. Each array is terminated by a zero integer.

Each file has an array of pointers to its index arrays. This array is terminated with a zero pointer.

The data base has an array of pointers to the index pointer arrays of the files. Each entry in this array represents one file. This array is an array of pointers to pointers to integer arrays. The array is terminated with a null pointer, and it must be named **index_ele**.

Listing 6.8 shows the arrays required to complete the CBS Cdata DDL.

Listing 6.8

```
/*
 *  Listing 6-8.  Index Specifications
 */

int clients_index_1 [] = {
    CLIENT_NO,
    0
};

int *clients_index [] = {
    clients_index_1,
    (int *) 0
};

int projects_index_1 [] = {
    PROJECT_NO,
    0
};

int *projects_index [] = {
    projects_index_1,
    (int *) 0
};

int consultants_index_1 [] = {
    CONSULTANT_NO,
    0
};

int *consultants_index [] = {
    consultants_index_1,
    (int *) 0
};

int assignments_index_1 [] = {
    CONSULTANT_NO,
    PROJECT_NO,
    0
};
```

continued...

...from previous page

```
int assignments_index_2 [] = {
    CONSULTANT_NO,
    0
};

int assignments_index_3 [] = {
    PROJECT_NO,
    0
};

int *assignments_index [] = {
    assignments_index_1,
    assignments_index_2,
    assignments_index_3,
    (int *) 0
};

int **index_ele [] = {
    clients_index,
    projects_index,
    consultants_index,
    assignments_index,
    (int **) 0
};
```

THE CDATA DDL COMPILER

The application of C language features to describe a data base schema to the DBMS software is an approach marked by its simplicity. It has been used in many applications since it was first developed, and C language has served its purpose well; however, when the data base becomes complex, the schema becomes difficult to manage. The proximity of items in their arrays is critical in this approach, and their order must be carefully maintained. If you add a data element to the dictionary, you must be careful to get its length in the proper place in the length array and its name in the proper place in the name array. If you add a file, you must carefully adjust the arrays that point to other arrays.

Because of the problems associated with maintaining a complex schema, it was decided that Cdata should use a compiled schema language. Listing 6.9 is the CBS schema coded in the CBS DDL. This schema is shorter and simpler than all the #defines, arrays, and structures of the DDL source code, yet it contains all the necessary components to describe the data base as it has been designed.

(Listing 6.9 on next page)

Listing 6.9 (cbs.sch)

```
; --------- cbs.sch    schema for consultant's billing system

; ------ data element dictionary

#schema CBS

#dictionary
    CLIENT_NO,       Z, 5,   "_____"
    CLIENT_NAME,     A, 25,  "_____"
    ADDRESS,         A, 25,  "_____"
    CITY,            A, 25,  "_____"
    STATE,           A, 2,   "__"
    ZIP,             N, 5,   "_____"
    PHONE,           N, 10,  "(___)___-____"
    AMT_DUE,         C, 8,   "$_____.__"
    PROJECT_NO,      Z, 5,   "_____"
    PROJECT_NAME,    A, 25,  "_____"
    AMT_EXPENDED,    C, 9,   "$_____.__"
    CONSULTANT_NO,   Z, 5,   "_____"
    CONSULTANT_NAME, A, 25,  "_____"
    RATE,            C, 5,   "$___.__"
    PAYMENT,         C, 9,   "$_____.__"
    EXPENSE,         C, 9,   "$_____.__"
    HOURS,           N, 2,   "__"
    DATE_PAID,       D, 6,   "__/__/__"
#end dictionary

; ---- file specifications

#file CLIENTS
    CLIENT_NO
    CLIENT_NAME
    ADDRESS
    CITY
    STATE
    ZIP
    PHONE
    AMT_DUE
    DATE_PAID
#end file
```

continued...

...from previous page

```
#file PROJECTS
    PROJECT_NO
    PROJECT_NAME
    AMT_EXPENDED
    CLIENT_NO
#end file

#file CONSULTANTS
    CONSULTANT_NO
    CONSULTANT_NAME
#end file

#file ASSIGNMENTS
    CONSULTANT_NO
    PROJECT_NO
    RATE
#end file

; ----- index specifications

#key CLIENTS      CLIENT_NO
#key PROJECTS     PROJECT_NO
#key CONSULTANTS CONSULTANT_NO
#key ASSIGNMENTS CONSULTANT_NO, PROJECT_NO
#key ASSIGNMENTS CONSULTANT_NO
#key ASSIGNMENTS PROJECT_NO

#end schema CBS
```

The language will be discussed first and then the program that compiles it. Throughout this discussion, refer to Listing 6.9 as an example.

THE CDATA DDL

The Cdata DDL is a text file that you can prepare with any text editor that produces ASCII files. It consists of lines of descriptive information about the data element dictionary, the files, and the indexes.

Comments

Any line that begins with a semicolon is a comment. The comment in a DDL is exactly like a comment in any other source language. Its purpose is to document the code for the human reader. The compiler ignores the comment.

DDL Directives

Directives begin with a pound sign (#) in column 1. One of several key phrases follows the pound sign. These phrases must appear in their proper order. The directives are as follows:

```
# schema
# dictionary
# end dictionary
# file
# end file
# key
# end schema
```

The first directive that appears in a Cdata DDL file is the **#schema** directive, which names the data base. At least one space or tab character and the data base name follow the directive. The compiler will use the data base name in comments in the compiled C language schema. The **#schema** directive cannot appear anywhere else in the file.

The **#end schema** directive is the last directive that must appear in a Cdata DDL file. It cannot appear anywhere else in the file.

Data Element Dictionary

The data element dictionary is the first part of the data base that you define. It begins with the **#dictionary** DDL directive and ends with the **#end dictionary** directive. The statements between the two directives describe the data elements. Each data element statement has four parts to describe the data element: its name, its data element type, its length, and its display mask. Commas separate the four parts. The name follows the C language convention for variable identifier, and the data element type is one of the following codes:

A　　= alphanumeric
C　　= currency
Z　　= numeric, zero-filled
N　　= numeric, space-filled
D　　= date

The data element length is an integer that expresses the data element's length without the null string terminator of the C language. Dates are six characters long, but other types can be any length you choose. The display mask is a string enclosed in double quotes, and the underscore character represents character positions in the mask. You can insert punctuation characters anywhere in the mask. The string for a date could be as follows:

"___/___/___"

You should include as many underscore characters as there are characters in the length of the data element. Even though you can assign any size to a data element, the system places a practical limit on the size of a display mask. You cannot display all of a data element if it is wider than your screen or printer. If you code a mask shorter than the data element, the data entry and display utility programs will concatenate the data element when they display it.

File Specifications

The Cdata DDL allows you to specify as many files as you want in a data base. File specifications begin with the **#file** directive, which names the file. The file name can be up to 31 characters and must obey the rules for C language identifiers. Since the PC-DOS names for the data and index files use the first 8 characters of the schema's file name, that file name must use PC-DOS file name conventions and must be unique from other file names in the first eight positions.

Each line in a file specification names a data element. The data element name must be one of those already defined in the data element dictionary.

You complete the specification of each file with the **#end file** directive.

Index Specifications

Index specifications tell Cdata which data elements to use for indexes in the files. The **#key** directive identifies an index specification, which is a single-line entry. You follow the **#key** directive keyword with a file name that you have already specified in a **#file** directive. You then follow the file name with one or more spaces. Finally, you list the data element name or names that make up the key. Where a key contains multiple data element names, you must separate the names with commas. Such a key definition becomes a concatenated key.

The first key named for a file is its **primary key**. Cdata will ensure that data values in a file's primary key data element are unique. Further, if the primary key data element appears in another file, Cdata relates the files. Cdata will not allow you to add a record to the other file unless its value for the data element is null or matched to a record in this file. As an example, with Cdata you cannot assign a project to a nonexistent client but you can establish a project before the client is known.

Nonprimary keys are **secondary keys**. These keys can have multiple values in the same file. So if you wanted to establish the data element **client__no** as a secondary key in the PROJECTS file, you could have more than one project record for the same client. But you could not establish more than one project record with the same project number since **project__no** is the primary key into the PROJECTS file.

THE CDATA DBMS HEADER SOURCE FILES

To compile most of the programs that follow in this and later chapters, you will need the source file named **cdata.h**. This file, shown in Listing 6.10, contains global definitions that you use throughout the system during compilation. You can change these definitions to suit your own application.

Cdata.h identifies the compiler that you use and causes the source code to adjust to the differences found between C compilers for the IBM PC. These differences are discussed in Chapter 9.

Cdata.h also defines the length of a B-tree node (discussed later in this chapter) with the **#define NODE** statement. You can change this length if you want to alter the size of the B-tree node. **Cdata.h** sets the type of a file address to the **long** integer with the **#define RPTR** statement, which allows a 32-bit file address, meaning that files can have up to 2^{32} records. If your files will each contain 64536 or fewer records, change this definition from **long** to **unsigned**.

Cdata.h defines the error codes that Cdata functions return. Remember the earlier discussion about the limitations placed by DBMS packages. Cdata also has limitations, but you can change them. The three global values, **MAXFILS**, **MAXELE**, and **MAXINDEX**, in **cdata.h** define the maximum number of files in a data base, the maximum number of data elements in a file, and the maximum number of indexes per file. The global symbol **MAXKEYLEN** establishes the maximum character size of a key data element or elements. If you change any of these global symbols, you must recompile the Cdata library module with the DML functions described later. **Cdata.h** also declares the Cdata schema external array formats for any program that will access them. Remember that you compile the schema separately and that Cdata and the applications and utility programs treat them as externally declared arrays. The declaration of these external arrays is done in **cdata.h** to locate them in a single source module.

Listing 6.10 (cdata.h)

```
/* --------------- cdata.h --------------------- */

#define AZTEC        1   /* Manx Aztec C86           */
#define CI_C86       2   /* Computer Innovations C86 */
#define DATALIGHT    3   /* Datalight C              */
#define ECOC         4   /* Eco-C88                  */
#define LATTICE      5   /* Lattice C                */
#define LETSC        6   /* Mark Williams Let's C    */
#define MICROSOFT    7   /* Microsoft C              */
#define TURBOC       8   /* Turbo C                  */
#define WIZARD       9   /* Wizard C                 */

#define ERROR -1
#define OK 0

#ifndef TRUE
#define TRUE 1
#define FALSE 0
#endif

#if COMPILER != LATTICE
#if COMPILER != LETSC
#if COMPILER != CI_C86
#include <errno.h>
#endif
#endif
#endif

#if COMPILER != LETSC
#if COMPILER != DATALIGHT
#if COMPILER != CI_C86
#include <fcntl.h>
#endif
#endif
#endif

#include <ctype.h>

extern int errno;
```

continued...

...from previous page

```
#if COMPILER == MICROSOFT
#include <sys\types.h>
#include <sys\stat.h>
#define OPENMODE O_RDWR+O_BINARY
#undef CMODE
#define CMODE S_IWRITE
#endif

#if COMPILER == TURBOC
#include <sys\stat.h>
#define OPENMODE O_RDWR+O_BINARY
#undef CMODE
#define CMODE S_IWRITE
#endif

#if COMPILER == CI_C86
#define void int
#define atol atoi
#undef CMODE
#define CMODE BUPDATE
#define OPENMODE BUPDATE
#endif

#if COMPILER == LETSC
#define CMODE 0
#define OPENMODE 2
#endif

#if COMPILER == DATALIGHT
#define CMODE 0
#define OPENMODE 2
#endif

#if COMPILER == WIZARD
#define CMODE 0x8080
#define OPENMODE O_RDWR+O_BINARY
#endif

#if COMPILER == LATTICE
#define OPENMODE O_RDWR
```

continued...

...from previous page

```
#define CMODE 0666
#endif

#if COMPILER == AZTEC
#define OPENMODE O_RDWR
#define CMODE 0666
#endif

#if COMPILER == ECOC
#define OPENMODE O_RDWR
#define CMODE 0
#endif

long lseek();

#define NODE 512        /* length of a B-tree node      */
#define RPTR long       /* B-tree node and file address */

#define MXFILS   11 /* maximum files in a data base    */
#define MXELE   100 /* maximum data elements in a file */
#define MXINDEX   5 /* maximum indexes per file        */

/* ----------- dbms error codes for errno return ------ */
#define D_NF       1 /* record not found               */
#define D_PRIOR    2 /* no prior record for this request */
#define D_EOF      3 /* end of file                    */
#define D_BOF      4 /* beginning of file              */
#define D_DUPL     5 /* primary key already exists     */
#define D_OM       6 /* out of memory                  */
#define D_INDXC    7 /* index corrupted                */
#define D_IOERR    8 /* i/o error                      */

#define MXKEYLEN 80 /* maximum key length for indexes */

#ifndef SCHEMA
/* --------- schema as built for the application --------- */
extern char *dbfiles [];        /* file names            */
extern char *denames [];        /* data element names    */
extern char *elmask  [];        /* data element masks    */
extern char eltype [];          /* data element types    */
```

continued...

...from previous page

```
extern int ellen [];            /* data element lengths */
extern int *file_ele [];        /* file data elements   */
extern int **index_ele [];      /* index data elements  */

void mov_mem(), set_mem(), fatal();
void cls_file();
void build_b();
void put_char(), clear_screen(), cursor();
void error_message(), clear_notice(), post_notice();

/* ------------- data base function definitions ---------- */
void db_open(),db_cls(),dberror(),init_rcd(),
    clrrcd(),rcd_fill(),build_index();

/* ---------- screen driver function definitions --------- */
void init_screen(),protect(),edit(),
    display_template(),tally(),put_field();
#endif

/* ---------- file header --------------- */
typedef struct fhdr {
    RPTR first_record;
    RPTR next_record;
    int record_length;
} FHEADER;
```

THE COMPILER, SCHEMA.C

Schema.c (Listing 6.11) is a three-pass program that reads the Cdata DDL and compiles it into a set of three C language source files that comply with the schema requirements of Cdata. If you were to run the three passes of **schema.c** with the CBS DDL in Listing 6.9 as input, they would produce three files containing the source files from Listings 6.1 through 6.8. The first file contains the data base record structure definitions and the **#define** statements for the data element and file names. The second file contains the string pointer arrays for file names, data element names, data element types, and display masks, which all support the query and report utilities and application programs that want to use screen drivers. The third file defines the arrays of record and index definitions that constitute the data base schema. You should include the first file in any program that links with Cdata so that you can use the global file and data element names in your calls to the Cdata DML functions. You should also compile the three files together into a single, relocatable object module and link it with your program and the DML functions.

To run **schema.c**, enter its name and tell it the names of the input and output files. Enter a switch on the command line to tell it which pass you are running and, therefore, which file to generate.

Following are the commands to tell **schema.c** to produce **cbs.c1**, **cbs.c2**, and **cbs.c3** as the three files of C language schema from the file **cbs.sch**.

```
C>schema <cbs.sch >cbs.c1 -1
C>schema <cbs.sch >cbs.c2 -2
C>schema <cbs.sch >cbs.c3 -3
```

Listing 6.11 (schema.c)

```
/* --------------- schema.c ------------------- */

/*  Read a file from the standard input.
 *  Write one of three schema files to the standard output
 *  depending on the runtime switch.
 *  If -1 is on the command line,
 *      the #define statements are built.
 *  If -2 is on the command line,
 *      the file of ascii strings for
 *      file and data element names is built.
 *  If -3 is on the command line,
 *  the data base schema array source file is built.
 */

#include <stdio.h>
#define SCHEMA
#include "cdata.h"

#define MXCAT 3 /* maximum elements concatenated per index */
#define NAMLEN 31

struct dict {                      /* data element dictionary  */
    char dename [NAMLEN+1]; /*  name                      */
    char detype;            /*  type                      */
    int delen;              /*  length                    */
    char *demask;           /*  display mask              */
} dc [MXELE];
int dectr = 0;                     /* data elements in dictionary */
int fctr = 0;                      /* files in data base         */
char filename [MXFILS] [NAMLEN+1]; /* file name strings   */
int fileele [MXFILS] [MXELE];       /* elements in files   */
int ndxele [MXFILS] [MXINDEX] [MXCAT]; /* indices         */

char word[NAMLEN+1];
char *malloc();
int lnctr = 0;  /* input stream line counter */
char ln [160];

/* -------- error messages ----------- */
char *ers[] = { "invalid name",                   /*  1 */
```

    continued...

...from previous page

```
                "invalid length",                /*  2 */
                "comma missing",                 /*  3 */
                "invalid data type",             /*  4 */
                "quote missing",                 /*  5 */
                "#schema missing",               /*  6 */
                "#<command> missing",            /*  7 */
                "unexpected end of file",        /*  8 */
                "duplicate file name",           /*  9 */
                "unknown data element",          /* 10 */
                "too many data elements",        /* 11 */
                "out of memory",                 /* 12 */
                "unknown file name",             /* 13 */
                "too many indices in file",      /* 14 */
                "too many elements in index",    /* 15 */
                "duplicate data element",        /* 16 */
                "too many files",                /* 17 */
                "invalid command line switch"    /* 18 */
};

void de_dict(), files(), keys(), schout(), defout(),
     lcase(), strout(), error(), get_line(), skip_white(),
     name_val(), numb_val(), expect_comma(), depart();
char *get_word();
#define iswhite(c) ((c)==' '||(c)=='\t')
#define REMARK ';'

/* ---------------- main program -------------- */
main(argc, argv)
int argc;
char *argv[];
{
    get_line();
    if (strncmp(ln, "#schema ", 8))
        error(6);
    else    {
        get_word(ln + 8);
        name_val();
        printf("\n/");
        printf("* ------------ %s ------------ */\n", word);
    }

    continued...
```

...from previous page

```
    get_line();
    while (strncmp(ln, "#end schema", 11))  {
        if (strncmp(ln, "#dictionary", 11) == 0)
            de_dict();
        else if (strncmp(ln, "#file ", 6) == 0)
            files();
        else if (strncmp(ln, "#key ", 5) == 0)
            keys();
        else
            error(7);
        get_line();
    }
    if (argc > 1)    {
        if (strcmp(argv[1], "-1") == 0)
            defout();
        else if (strcmp(argv[1], "-2") == 0)
            strout();
        else if (strcmp(argv[1], "-3") == 0)
            schout();
        else
            error(18);
    }
    else
        error(18);
    depart(0);
}

/* -------- build the data element dictionary ---------- */
static void de_dict()
{
    char *cp, *cp1;
    int el;
    while (TRUE)    {
        get_line();
        if (strncmp(ln, "#end dictionary", 15) == 0)
            break;
        if (dectr == MXELE) {
            error(11);
            continue;
        }
```

continued...

...from previous page

```
        cp = get_word(ln);
        name_val();
        for (el = 0; el < dectr; el++)
            if (strcmp(word, dc[el].dename) == 0)    {
                error(16);
                continue;
            }
        strcpy(dc[dectr].dename, word);
        expect_comma(&cp);
        skip_white(&cp);
        switch (*cp)      {
            case 'A':
            case 'Z':
            case 'C':
            case 'N':
            case 'D':    break;
            default :    error(4);
                         continue;
        }
        dc[dectr].detype = *cp++;
        expect_comma(&cp);
        cp = get_word(cp);
        numb_val();
        dc[dectr].delen = atoi(word);
        expect_comma(&cp);
        skip_white(&cp);
        if (*cp != '"') {
            error(5);
            continue;
        }
        cp1 = cp + 1;
        while (*cp1 != '"' && *cp1 && *cp1 != '\n')
            cp1++;
        if (*cp1++ != '"')   {
            error(5);
            continue;
        }
        *cp1 = '\0';
        if ((dc[dectr].demask = malloc((cp1-cp)+1)) == 0)    {
            error(12);
```

continued...

...from previous page

```
            depart(1);
        }
        strcpy(dc[dectr].demask, cp);
        dectr++;
    }
}


/* ----------- build the file definitions ---------------- */
static void files()
{
    int i, el = 0;
    if (fctr == MXFILS)
        error(17);
    get_word(ln + 6);                    /* get the file name   */
    name_val();                          /* validate it         */
    for (i = 0; i < fctr; i++)      /* already assigned?   */
        if (strcmp(word, filename[i]) == 0)
            error(9);
    strcpy(filename[fctr], word);
    /* ---------- process the file's data elements -------- */
    while (TRUE)    {
        get_line();
        if (strncmp(ln, "#end file", 9) == 0)
            break;
        if (el == MXELE)    {
            error(11);
            continue;
        }
        get_word(ln);                    /* get a data element */
        for (i = 0; i < dectr; i++)  /* in dictionary?     */
            if (strcmp(word, dc[i].dename) == 0)
                break;
        if (i == dectr)
            error(10);
        else if (fctr < MXFILS)
            fileele [fctr] [el++] = i + 1; /* post to file */
    }
    if (fctr < MXFILS)
        fctr++;
}
```

continued...

...from previous page

```
/* ----------- build the index descriptions ------------ */
static void keys()
{
    char *cp;
    int f, el, x, cat = 0;
    cp = get_word(ln + 5);          /* get the file name */
    for (f = 0; f < fctr; f++)  /* in the schema?     */
        if (strcmp(word, filename[f]) == 0)
            break;
    if (f == fctr)  {
        error(13);
        return;
    }
    for (x = 0; x < MXINDEX; x++)
        if (*ndxele [f] [x] == 0)
            break;
    if (x == MXINDEX)    {
        error(14);
        return;
    }
    while (cat < MXCAT) {
        cp = get_word(cp);                  /* get index name */
        for (el = 0; el < dectr; el++)  /* in dictionary? */
            if (strcmp(word, dc[el].dename) == 0)
                break;
        if (el == dectr)    {
            error(10);
            break;
        }
        ndxele [f] [x] [cat++] = el + 1; /* post element */
        skip_white(&cp);
        if (*cp++ != ',')               /* concatenated index? */
            break;
        if (cat == MXCAT)    {
            error(15);
            break;
        }
    }
}
```

continued...

...from previous page

```
/* ---------- write the schema source language ---------- */
static void schout()
{
    int f, el, x, x1, cat, fel;
    char name [NAMLEN+1];

    /* --------- data element lengths ---------- */
    printf("\n\nint ellen [] = {");
    for (el = 0; el < dectr; el++)        {
        if ((el % 25) == 0)
            printf("\n\t");
        printf((el < dectr-1 ? "%d," : "%d"),dc[el].delen);
    }
    printf("\n};\n");
    /* ---------- write the file contents arrays ------- */
    for (f = 0; f < fctr; f++)   {
        lcase(name, filename [f]);
        printf("\n\nint f_%s [] = {", name);
        el = 0;
        while ((fel = fileele[f] [el++]) != 0)
            printf("\n\t%s,", dc[fel-1].dename);
        printf("\n\t0\n};");
    }
    /* ------- write the file list pointer array ------- */
    printf("\n\nint *file_ele [] = {");
    for (f = 0; f < fctr; f++)   {
        lcase(name, filename [f]);
        printf("\n\tf_%s,", name);
    }
    printf("\n\t0\n};\n");
    /* ---------- write the index arrays -------------- */
    for (f = 0; f < fctr; f++)   {
        lcase(name, filename [f]);
        for (x = 0; x < MXINDEX; x++)    {
            if (*ndxele [f] [x] == 0)
                break;
            printf("\nint x%d_%s [] = {", x + 1, name);
            for (cat = 0; cat < MXCAT; cat++)
                if (ndxele [f] [x] [cat])
```

continued...

...from previous page

```
                    printf("\n\t%s,",
                        dc[ndxele [f] [x] [cat] - 1].dename);
            printf("\n\t0\n};\n");
        }
        printf("\nint *x_%s [] = {", name);
        for (x1 = 0; x1 < x; x1++)
            printf("\n\tx%d_%s,", x1 + 1, name);
        printf("\n\t0\n};\n");
    }
    printf("\nint **index_ele [] = {");
    for (f = 0; f < fctr; f++)  {
        lcase(name, filename [f]);
        printf("\n\tx_%s,", name);
    }
    printf("\n\t0\n};\n");
}




/* -- write the schema #defines and struct definitions -- */
static void defout()
{
    int f, el, fel;
    char name [NAMLEN+1];

    /*  --------  data element defines  ---------  */
    for (el = 0; el < dectr; el++)
        printf("\n#define %s %d", dc[el].dename, el + 1);
    putchar('\n');
    /*  -------  write the file #define statements --------  */
    for (f = 0; f < fctr; f++)
        printf("\n#define %s %d", filename [f], f);
    putchar('\n');
    /*  ----------  write the record structures ------------  */
    for (f = 0; f < fctr; f++)  {
        lcase(name, filename [f]);
        printf("\nstruct %s {", name);
        el = 0;
        while ((fel = fileele[f] [el++]) != 0)  {
```

continued...

...from previous page

```
            lcase(name, dc[fel-1].dename);
            printf("\n\tchar %s [%d];",
                    name, dc[fel-1].delen + 1);
        }
        printf("\n};\n");
    }
}

/* ----- write the file and data element ascii strings ---- */
static void strout()
{
    int el, f;

    /* -------- data element ascii names --------- */
    printf("\nchar *denames [] = {");
    for (el = 0; el < dectr; el++)
        printf("\n\t\"%s\",", dc[el].dename);
    printf("\n\t0\n};\n");
    /* -------- data element types ------------ */
    printf("\nchar eltype [] = \"");
    for (el = 0; el < dectr; el++)
        putchar(dc[el].detype);
    printf("\";\n");
    /* ---------- data element display masks --------- */
    printf ("\nchar *elmask [] = {");
    for (el = 0; el < dectr; el++)
        printf((el < dectr-1 ?
                "\n\t%s," :
                "\n\t%s"),dc[el].demask);
    printf("\n};\n");
    /* ------ write the ascii file name strings -------- */
    printf("\nchar *dbfiles [] = {");
    for (f = 0; f < fctr; f++)
        printf("\n\t\"%s\",", filename [f]);
    printf("\n\t0\n};\n");
}
```

continued...

...from previous page

```c
/* -------- convert a name to lower case --------- */
static void lcase(s1, s2)
char *s1, *s2;
{
    while (*s2) {
        *s1 = tolower(*s2);
        s1++;
        s2++;
    }
    *s1 = '\0';
}


/* ----------- errors -------------- */
static void error(n)
int n;
{
    static int erct = 0;
    static int erlin = 0;

    if (erlin != lnctr) {
        erlin = lnctr;
        fprintf(stderr, "\nLine %d: %s", lnctr, ln);
    }
    fprintf(stderr, "\n  Error %d: %s", n, ers[n-1]);
    if (erct++ == 5)      {
        erct =0;
        fprintf(stderr, "\nContinue? (y/n) ... ");
        if (tolower(getc(stderr)) != 'y')
            depart(1);
    }
}


/* --- get a line of data from the schema input stream --- */
static void get_line()
{
    *ln = '\0';
    while (*ln == '\0' || *ln == REMARK || *ln == '\n') {
        if (fgets(ln,120,stdin) == 0)    {
            error(8);
            depart(1);
```

continued...

...from previous page

```
        }
        lnctr++;
    }
}

/* ---------- skip over white space --------- */
static void skip_white(s)
char **s;
{
    while (iswhite(**s))
        (*s)++;
}

/* ----------- get a word from a line of input ----------- */
static char *get_word(cp)
char *cp;
{
    int wl = 0, fst = 0;

    skip_white(&cp);
    while (*cp && *cp != '\n' &&
            *cp != ',' &&
                iswhite(*cp) == 0)  {
        if (wl == NAMLEN && fst == 0)   {
            error(1);
            fst++;
        }
        else
            word [wl++] = *cp++;
    }
    word [wl] = '\0';
    return cp;
}

/* ---------- validate a name --------------- */
static void name_val()
{
    char *s = word;
    if (isalpha(*s))    {
        while (isalpha(*s) || isdigit(*s) || *s == '_') {
```

continued...

...from previous page

```
            *s = toupper(*s);
            s++;
        }
        if (*s == '\0')
            return;
    }
    error(1);
}

/* ---------- validate a number ------------- */
static void numb_val()
{
    char *s = word;
    do  {
        if (isdigit(*s++) == 0) {
            error(2);
            break;
        }
    } while (*s);
}

/* ----------- expect a comma next ---------- */
static void expect_comma(cp)
char **cp;
{
    skip_white(cp);
    if (*(*cp)++ != ',')
        error(3);
}

/* --------- terminate schema program ------------- */
static void depart(n)
int n;
{
    int el;

    for (el = 0; el < dectr; el++)
        free(dc[el].demask);
    exit(n);
}
```

continued...

...from previous page

```
#if COMPILER == WIZARD
/* --- strncmp function to replace non-standard version --- */
int strncmp(s1, s2, n)
char *s1, *s2;
{
    int i;

    while (n--)
        if (i = (*s1++ - *s2++))
            return i;
    return 0;
}
#endif
```

Schema.c is an example of a program that uses some of the standard features of the C language and PC-DOS. It is a simple compiler that compiles DDL statements into C statements, and it uses a combination of PC-DOS command line arguments and input/output redirection. In the three commands shown previously, you can see that each of the three passes of **schema.c** uses the file named **cbs.sch** as its input. Since the program reads the DDL statements from the standard input device, you specify the file name on the command line when you run the program. Then, since the program writes its compiled output to the standard output device, you specify the output file as the standard output device on the command line. With PC-DOS, you name the standard input and output devices on the command line with the less-than and greater-than symbols (< and >). When you follow this convention, the program can use the standard C input/output functions to read its input and write its results. Notice that all messages to the operator are written to the **stderr** device so they will appear on the operator's console rather than in the file name you assigned to **stdout**.

Schema.c uses the C language **argc, argv** command line parameter convention to allow the operator to specify which of the three passes is being run. Specify them as the -1, -2, and -3 entries on the command line, as the examples show. You will find a description of **argc** and **argv** on page 110 of *The C Programming Language* (Kernighan and Ritchie, Prentice Hall, 1978). Most C compilers have adopted this command line argument convention. Note how **schema.c** uses it toward the end of the **main** function where the program tests for the three parameter values.

Schema.c is rigorous in its syntax checking. Earlier, you learned the Cdata DDL syntax. The compiler makes sure that you stick to the rules. If you code some bad syntax, the compiler delivers an appropriate error message and keeps running. The error message identifies the line number of the DDL file where the program found the error and displays the offending DDL statement and the compiler's complaint about the statement. Since one error could cause more errors to occur, the compiler pauses every five errors and asks if you want to keep going. You might find it more productive to quit, correct the errors, and restart the compiler.

Following is a list of the compiler's error messages and their meanings.

Error 1: invalid name

You have coded a file or data element name that is incorrect. Names must begin with letters and may contain letters and digits.

Error 2: invalid length

The specification of a data element length is not all digits.

Error 3: comma missing

A comma is missing where one is expected.

Error 4: invalid data type

The data type for a data element is not one of the following: A, Z, C, N, or D.

Error 5: quote missing

The display mask for a data element is not bound by double quotation marks. Either the beginning mark or the terminating mark is missing.

Error 6: #schema missing

The compiler did not find the **#schema** statement where it expected it to be.

Error 7: # <command> missing

The compiler has expected to find either a **#dictionary**, a **#file**, or a **#key** DDL statement and found none of these.

Error 8: unexpected end of file

The compiler has reached the end of file on the DDL statement file without reaching a logical end to the specification of the data base.

Error 9: duplicate file name

You have given two files the same name.

Error 10: unknown data element

You have specified a data element in a file that is not in the data element dictionary.

Error 11: too many data elements

The number of data elements in your schema exceeds the value assigned to the global symbol **MXELE** at the start of the source file for schema.c.

Error 12: out of memory

The compiler has run out of memory while attempting to allocate a buffer.

Error 13: unknown file name

The index specification names a file that does not appear in the file specifications.

Error 14: too many indices in file

You have assigned more keys to a file than the global symbol **MXIN-DEX** specifies. You will find **MXINDEX** defined at the beginning of the source file for schema.c.

Error 15: too many data elements in file

You have given more data elements to a file than the global symbol **MXELE** specifies. You will find **MXEXE** defined at the beginning of the source file for schema.c.

Error 16: duplicate data element

Two data elements in the dictionary have the same name.

Error 17: too many files

You have more files in your data base than the global symbol **MXFILS** specifies. You will find **MXFILS** defined at the beginning of the source file for schema.c.

Error 18: invalid cammand line switch

The command line parameter that tells the compiler which pass to run is not one of the following: -1, -2, or -3.

APPLICATION SOFTWARE ARCHITECTURE

Now that you have designed a data base and built its schema, you are ready for some applications programs to process some data. You will now design a program that prints invoices for clients from the data in the CLIENTS file of the CBS data base. This program will use some of the functions of the Cdata DML, which haven't been covered yet since they are described later in this chapter. This example is meant to show you how your programs will incorporate the schema and link with the Cdata functions.

Listing 6.12 is the **invoice.c** program. To run the program, type its name, **invoice**. Since the invoice data is sent to **stdout**, you must redirect it to the printer as shown here:

    A>invoice >prn

For the program to do anything, you must have some data in the CLIENTS file. Later, after have loaded data and posted transactions, you will integrate this program into a complete billing system. But for now, since it is small, you can use it to see how to connect to the Cdata DDL.

(Listing 6.12 on next page)

Listing 6.12 (invoice.c)

```
/* ------------------ invoice.c --------------------- */

/*
 * produce invoices from the clients file
 */

#include <stdio.h>
#include "cdata.h"
#include "cbs.c1"

struct clients cl;

main()
{
    static int fl [] = {CLIENTS, -1};
    double atof();

    db_open("", fl);
    while (TRUE)     {
        if (next_rcd(CLIENTS, 1, &cl) == ERROR)
            break;
        printf("\n\n\nInvoice for Services Rendered\n");
        printf("\n%s", cl.client_name);
        printf("\n%s", cl.address);
        printf("\n%s, %s %s", cl.city, cl.state, cl.zip);
        printf("\n\nAmount Due: $%10.2f\n",
                    atof(cl.amt_due) / 100);
    }
    db_cls();
}
```

The **#include** statements at the top of the listing connect you to the
DDL for the CBS data base. The first one, **stdio.h**, is a standard C
header file. The next header file is **cdata.h**, which was explained earlier
in this chapter.

The file **cbs.c1** is the schema for CBS. You will always include its counterpart in a program that uses Cdata. It has the **#define** statements for the data element and file names. It also defines the structures that describe each of the records in the data base. This file is one of three that are generated by **schema.c**, the schema compiler.

The structure of type **clients** is included as part of the CBS schema in **cbs.c1**. You will have a similar structure for each file in your data base. The schema defines the structures. You must declare variables of the structures to reserve memory for buffers.

Note the uses of the global symbol **CLIENTS**. The schema defines **CLIENTS** as an integer that is equated to the CLIENTS file. The Cdata functions will use that integer to subscript into the arrays that describe the CLIENTS file.

The **printf** statements use members of the structure named **cl** to address data elements in the record buffer. These names come from the data element dictionary and are in lowercase, which will differentiate them from the same names in uppercase that define the data element integer values.

The calls to **db_open**, **next_rcd**, and **db_cls** represent the Data Manipulation Language interface between the application program and the data base manager.

After you learn all the Cdata functions and begin coding, you will see that this little program has everything needed to connect an application program to the schema. If you include the proper files and link the program with the Cdata library, you will have built a fully functioning, single-user data base management system into your own software.

CDATA FILE FORMATS

This discussion covers the format and architecture of files and indexes in a data base built with the Cdata functions. You do not need an understanding of these internal formats to use Cdata, but it can help you in deciding whether to use this approach for a particular application. And, if you want to integrate the data with other software, you will need to know what it looks like.

Data Files

Each data base file described in the Cdata DDL has a corresponding disk file. The file name comes from the first eight characters of the data base file name as expressed in the DDL **#file** directive. The file extension is always .DAT. With this naming convention, you can see how the CLIENTS file in the CBS data base gets its name, CLIENTS.DAT.

A file consists of a header record followed by a series of fixed-length data records. The header record is the same length and format for all files, but the data record length depends on the data element composition of the file.

Following is the format of the header record:

```
struct fhdr    {        /* header on each file */
    RPTR first_record; /* first available deleted record */
    RPTR next_record;  /* next available record position */
    int record_length; /* length of record */
};
```

A **typedef** in the header file cdata.h equates the variable type **RPTR** to either **unsigned** or **long**. Which type you use will depend on the number of records you can support in a file. An **unsigned RPTR** will support 65536 records, and a **long RPTR** will support 2^{32} records. The length of the file header record will depend on the **RPTR** definition. For an **unsigned RPTR**, the record is 6 characters long. For a **long RPTR,** the record is 10 characters long.

Two variables in the file header record contain the file's current length and its record length. A third variable controls the file's reusable deleted record space. Deleting a record adds the space it occupies to a reusable record-linked list. The **RPTR** variable **first__record** points to the first of these spaces. The records themselves are marked with a delete flag, and each one points to the next record in the list. The delete mark occupies the first **RPTR** space in the record and is set to the value -1. The list pointer in the record uses the second **RPTR** space in the record and contains the record number of the next available deleted record. Records are added to and taken from the beginning of the list. Record numbers are relative to one.

Reusable deleted record space eliminates the need to pack or compress the data file to clean up the deleted records.

A data record in a file is equal in length to the sum of the lengths of the data elements plus one for each data element for the null string terminator.

Cdata stores data values in files as null-terminated ASCII strings, regardless of the data types. Numbers may or may not have leading zeros. Currency fields are stored without the decimal point. Dates have six characters in month, day, year format.

Cdata stores new records in the first available record space from the deleted record list or at the end of the file. Initially, the file contains only the file header record; the physical file size grows as Cdata adds records.

Index Files

Cdata supports the relational data model with inverted indexes into data files. The inverted index processes use B-tree algorithms.

The **B-tree** is an index structure that R. Bayer and E. McCreight developed in 1970. It is a balanced tree of key values used to locate the data file record that matches a specified key argument. The tree is a hierarchy of nodes where each node contains from one to a fixed number of keys.

A B-tree consists of a **root node** and two or more lower nodes. If the total number of keys in the tree is equal to or less than the number that a node can contain, then only the root node exists. When that number exceeds the capacity of a node, the root node splits into two lower nodes, retaining the key that is logically between the key values of the two new nodes. Higher nodes are **parents** of the lower nodes. Nodes store keys in key value sequence. When the tree has multiple levels, each key in a parent node points to the lower node that contains keys greater than the parent key and less than the next adjacent key in the parent. The nodes at the lowest level are called **leaves**. The keys in a leaf node point to the file records that match the indexed values. Since values occur at all levels in the tree, the first key in a leaf is preceded by a pointer to the record of a key value from a higher node.

Figure 6.3 is an example of a B-tree that uses the letters of the alphabet as keys to locate matching words from the phonetic alphabet used by airplane pilots. The letters are analogous to the data values for key data elements in a file; the list of phonetic alphabet words is similar to the file records that the B-tree indexes.

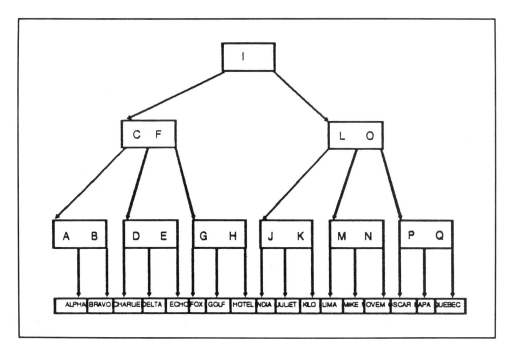

Figure 6.3   The B-Tree

When a node becomes overpopulated by key value insertions, the insertion algorithm splits it into two nodes and inserts the middle key value into the parent node of the original presplit node. If the root node splits, a new root node is grown as the parent of the split nodes.

When a node becomes underpopulated as the result of key value deletions, it combines with an adjacent node. The key value that is between the two nodes and that is in the common parent node of the two is moved into the combined node and deleted from the parent node. If the deleted key is the last key in the root node, then the old root node is deleted, and the newly combined node becomes the root node.

In the example in Figure 6.3, the root node has one key value, and the other nodes each have two keys. This example makes for a simple illustration of the structure, but, in actual practice, a typical B-tree will have as many keys in a node as are practical. The arrows in the figure represent actual record pointers that point to lower nodes in the tree or, in the leaf nodes, point to the records in the file being indexed.

The B-tree algorithms provide that the tree always remains in balance; that is, the number of levels from the root node to the bottom of the tree is always the same no matter which branch is taken by the search. This property gives the B-tree its name. The "B" stands for "balanced."

Cdata uses the B-tree algorithms to build and maintain inverted index files, one for each **#key** directive in the DDL. The index file name is the same as the data file name taken from the DDL **#file** directive. Cdata builds the file extension, which will be .X01 for the first index into the file, .X02 for the second, and so on. The client number index for the CLIENTS file in the CBS data base is named CLIENTS.X01. The primary key index into a file always has a file extension of .X01. The maintenance of these index B-trees is transparent to the applications software.

Each B-tree file contains a header record followed by the nodes. The global symbol **NODE** found in the file **cdata.h** defines the length of a node. The header and all nodes have this length. The format of the header can be seen as the structure **tree__hdr** in the source file **btree.c** later in this chapter. It contains the key length, the address of the root node, the number of keys that a node can contain, a pointer to the next available node that can be added to the file, and a pointer to the last node that was deleted from the tree.

The format of the nodes is described in the structure **treenode**, also in **btree.c**. Each node contains a flag that identifies the node as a leaf or a nonleaf, pointers to the parent and left and right sibling nodes, and the node/file pointers and key values.

CDATA SYSTEM ARCHITECTURE

Cdata manages a data base that consists of data files and B-tree index files. Figure 6.4 shows the layers of software that combine to provide this support.

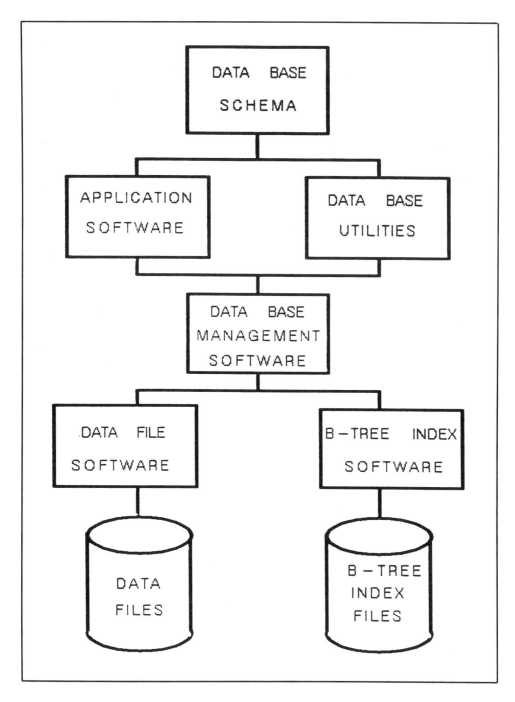

Figure 6.4   The Cdata System Architecture

At the bottom of Figure 6.4 are the data and index files. Data files are managed by a set of software functions that are dedicated to file management. Index files are managed by a different software function set. The two sets of functions are unrelated, and the files themselves are unconnected. These functions are unseen by the programs that you write in support of your application.

Above the data file and index file software is a library of functions whose purpose is to manage the data base. Since the data base is a collection of data and index files, the data base management functions call the data file and index file management functions directly. The data base maintains the relationship that logically exists among the many files that constitute the data base. This set of functions represents the Cdata Data Manipulation Language (DML).

Above the data base management software are two sets of programs: your applications software and the Cdata data base utility programs. These programs are concerned with files in the data base. It would seem that they deal primarily with data files, but they use index files as well. Their access to the data base is provided by the higher-level language of the DML.

Above everything is the schema that describes the actual data base that Cdata is managing for the application and the utility programs.

CDATA: THE DATA MANIPULATION LANGUAGE FUNCTIONS

Now that you can describe a data base using the Cdata DDL, you will want to write programs that can process data records. Your programs need to add records, retrieve records, change records, and delete records. The C functions that follow serve those purposes and provide some utility functions related to data base management. These functions constitute what is sometimes called the **host language interface** because they allow the host programming language (C, in this case) to connect with the DBMS. **Data Manipulation Language (DML)** is the Cdata name for these functions.

You compile applications programs with the data base schema and link them with the DML functions. Then the applications programs call the DML functions by using the mnemonic file and data element names of the schema. The DML functions operate on the files as described by the schema.

Function db_open:

```
db_open(path, fl)
char *path;    /* DOS path where the data base is
int *fl;       /* file list               */
```

The **db_open** function is the first one you call to use the Cdata function toolset. Its purpose is to initialize the data base files and their index files for access by your programs. You pass it a PC-DOS path to the data base and the address of an array of integers representing a list of the file numbers you will be accessing. The path is a fully qualified PC-DOS path specification including the drive designation. If, for example, the data base is on the B drive under the subdirectory named \cbs, the call to **db_open** will look like this:

```
static int list[] = {CLIENTS, PROJECTS, -1};

db_open("b:\\cbs\\", list);
```

Db_open will append file names to the path specifier you send it, so make sure you include the terminating double-backslash if you pass a subdirectory in the path. Be aware that some PC-DOS implementations use the SWITCHAR option in their CONFIG.SYS startup command file. The SWITCHAR option allows the user to redefine the path specifier character from the backslash to something else. Most experts will discourage this practice. While it is possible for a program to find the current SWITCHAR setting from the DOS environment string, most programs don't bother, and future versions of DOS will probably eliminate the option.

The file name array must be terminated with the integral value -1. Usually, a program will initialize its array with the global file names defined in the Cdata data definition language as seen in the example above.

Db__open does not return a value. It expects valid file numbers in the list you pass. As long as you use the global file name convention, you will have no problem with file numbers. If the data base is always located on the default drive in the current subdirectory, pass a null string for the **path** parameter as in this example:

```
db_open("", list);
```

Function add_rcd:

```
int add_rcd(f, bf)
int f;          /* file number                */
char *bf;       /* buffer containing record */
```

Use this function to add a record to a file. Pass it the file number and a pointer to the buffer containing the new record's data. **Add__rcd** will return **OK** if it finds no errors. If it returns **ERROR**, the global variable **errno** will contain a code describing the error. One error code you can get is **D__DUPL** (duplicate key, as defined in **cdata.h**). This code says that the record contains a primary key value that is assigned to another record. The code **D__NF** says that one of the data elements in the record is the primary key index data element for another file; the other file has no record keyed on the value in the record that you are adding.

Function find_rcd:

```
int find_rcd(f,k,key,bf)
int f;          /* file number           */
int k;          /* key number            */
char *key;      /* key value             */
char *bf;       /* buffer for record     */
```

This function is the first of several that you use to retrieve records from the data base. The file number is required — use one of the globally defined file names. The key number is an integer relative to one that specifies which of the indexes you will use. If you are searching the primary index, then pass the value 1 as the key number parameter. The number of the key is the relative position of the key in the schema definition array. The second key is number 2; the third is number 3, and so on. The character pointer named **key** points to the buffer in the caller's space where the retrieval will store the data record (if it finds one).

The function will return **OK** if it finds a record that matches the key value in the key data element. If the function cannot find a record, it returns **ERROR** with the code **D__NF** in errno.

Function verify_rcd:

```
int verify_rcd(f,k,key)
int f;        /* file number       */
int k;        /* key number        */
char *key;    /* key value         */
```

This function is similar to **find__rcd** except that it does not retrieve a record. Its purpose is to verify that a particular record exists. You use this function when you want to know if a record is in the data base, but you do not need the record's contents. You might use this function to validate the presence of an item needed by your processing. Its calling parameters are the same as for **find__rcd** except that you do not provide a record buffer when you call the function.

If the record exists, the function returns **OK**; otherwise, it returns **ERROR**, and **D__NF** is in **errno**.

Function first_rcd:

```
int first_rcd(f,k,bf)
int f;        /* file number       */
int k;        /* key number        */
char *bf;     /* buffer for record */
```

You use the function **first_rcd** to retrieve the first record from a file based on the sequence of the index specified by the key number. You pass the file number, the key number, and a pointer to the buffer where the function should write the record that it retrieves.

If the function returns **OK**, it located a record and placed it in the buffer. If the function returns **ERROR**, no records exist in the file, and the value **D_EOF** (end of file) is in errno.

Function last_rcd:

```
int last_rcd(f,k,bf)
int f;          /* file number          */
int k;          /* key number           */
char *bf;       /* buffer for record    */
```

The function **last_rcd** is the reverse of **first_rcd**. You use it to retrieve the last record from a file based on the sequence of the index specified by the key number. As with **first_rcd**, you pass the file number, the key number, and a pointer to the buffer where the function is to write the record it retrieves.

If the function returns **OK**, it located a record and placed it in the buffer. If the function returns **ERROR**, no records exist in the file, and the value **D_BOF** (beginning of file) is in **errno**.

Function next_rcd:

```
int next_rcd(f,k,bf)
int f;          /* file number          */
int k;          /* key number           */
char *bf;       /* buffer for record    */
```

You use the function **next_rcd** to retrieve the next record from a file based on the sequence of the index specified by the key number parameter. If no prior access has been made to the file through the same index, then this function behaves exactly like **first_rcd**. You pass the file number, the key number, and a pointer to the buffer where the function is to write the record. If the function returns **OK**, it located a record and placed it in the buffer.

Successive calls to **next_rcd** will deliver the records in the ascending sequence of the index.

If the function returns **ERROR**, no records exist in the file past the current record in the chosen sequence, and the value **D_EOF** (end of file) is in **errno**.

Function prev_rcd:

```
int prev_rcd(f,k,bf)
int f;          /* file number          */
int k;          /* key number           */
char *bf;       /* buffer for record    */
```

The function **prev_rcd** is the opposite of **next_rcd**, and you use it to retrieve the previous record from a file based on the sequence of the index specified by the key number parameter. If no prior access has been made to the file through the same index, then this function behaves exactly like **last_rcd**. You pass the file number, the key number, and a pointer to the buffer where the function is to write the record. If the function returns **OK**, it located a record and wrote it in the buffer.

Successive calls to **prev_rcd** will deliver the records in the descending sequence of the index.

If the function returns **ERROR**, no prior records exist in the file, and the value **D_BOF** (beginning of file) is in **errno**.

Function rtn_rcd:

```
int rtn_rcd(f,bf)
int f;        /* file number            */
char *bf;     /* buffer containing record */
```

Use this function to return a record that was previously retrieved by one of the functions **find_rcd**, **first_rcd**, **last_rcd**, **next_rcd**, **prev_rcd**, and **seqrcd**. Pass it the file number and a pointer to the buffer containing the record's new data.

If **rtn_rcd** finds no errors, it will return **OK**. If it returns **ERROR**, the global variable **errno** will contain a code that identifies the error. One possible error code is **D_DUPL** (duplicate key). As it does in **add_rcd**, this code says that the record contains a primary key value that is already assigned to another record in the file. This situation can occur if you change the value of the primary key data element to a value already in use. It is also possible to receive the error code **D_PRIOR** (no prior record), which will happen if you have not previously retrieved a record using one of the retrieval functions. The error code **D_NF** may also appear if one of the data elements in the record is the primary key index data element for another file; the other file has no record keyed on the value that is in the new record.

Function del_rcd:

```
int del_rcd(f)
int f;        /* file number            */
```

You will use this function to delete a record that was previously retrieved by one of the functions **find_rcd**, **first_rcd**, **last_rcd**, **next_rcd**, **prev_rcd**, and **seqrcd**. Pass it the file number.

If **del_rcd** finds no errors, it will return **OK**. If it returns **ERROR**, the global variable **errno** will contain a code that identifies the error. One possible error code is **D_PRIOR** (no prior record), which will happen if you have not previously retrieved a record using one of the retrieval functions.

Function seqrcd:

```
int seqrcd(f,bf)
int f;       /* file number         */
char *bf;    /* buffer for record   */
```

This function retrieves records from a file in their physical sequence in the file. Pass it the file number and a pointer to the record buffer.

The function bypasses deleted records and returns **OK** if it finds a record. If it finds no record, it returns **ERROR,** and **D__EOF** is in **errno**.

Function db_cls:

```
db_cls()
```

Call **db__cls** to close all data base files, flush the buffers, and close the index files. Do not forget to call this function. If you leave it out, any changed data will be unreliable, and the indexes will be locked.

Function dberror:

```
dberror()
```

This function is a utility you can call whenever any of the Cdata functions discussed in this chapter returns the value **ERROR**. **dberror** displays a message indicating the cause of the error. The message displayed is based on the value in the global variable **errno**. If the error is a programming violation of the rules of Cdata, **dberror** will abort the program; otherwise, it will return to the caller. This function provides a convenient way to let Cdata handle your error messages.

Function rcd_fill:

```
rcd_fill(s,d,slist,dlist)
char *s;        /* source record buffer        */
char *d;        /* destination record buffer   */
int *slist;     /* source data element list    */
int *dlist;     /* destination data element list */
```

This function is the Cdata equivalent of COBOL's **MOVE COR-RESPONDING** verb. You use it to move groups of data elements from one record to another. In COBOL, if you use **MOVE CORRESPOND-ING** to move one data structure to another, only the data items with like names are moved. Data elements that are in the source record and not in the destination are not moved, and data items that are in the destination record but not in the source are not disturbed.

Cdata defines records as sequences of data elements; data element names are integers, and records are represented by arrays of data element integers. Given two record descriptions and two buffer addresses, it is possible to use the data element lengths from the dictionary to find the relative locations of common data elements in both buffers; then, the data values from the source record can be moved to the data elements in the destination record. The **rcd_fill** function performs this process.

Suppose you are retrieving records from the PROJECTS file in the CBS data base. Your retrieval does not require all the data elements from the record. Only the project name and the amount expended are required. It is possible to describe a record with an array of data element name integers and then allow the functions of Cdata to manage that record's format for you. The code might look like this:

```
static int rlist[]={PROJECT_NAME, AMT_EXPENDED, 0};
char rcd [36];
struct projects pr;
    .
rcd_fill(&pr, rcd, file_ele[PROJECTS], rlist);
    .
```

Assume that at the time of the **rcd__fill** call you have retrieved a data record from the PROJECTS file into the structure named **pr**. You pass the addresses of the two lists and the addresses of the two buffers to the **rcd__fill** function. (One list, **rlist**, is special to this process; the other, **file__ele[PROJECTS]**, is a part of the data base schema.) When the function returns, the two data elements from the file are in the buffer named **rcd**.

Function epos:

```
epos(el, list)
int el;              /* data element */
int *list;           /* element list */
```

This function returns the relative character position of a data element in a buffer that has its format described by the data element list. The list is an array of integers that represent data elements as defined by the Cdata schema. If the data element integer passed as the first parameter is not in the list (or is zero), then the function returns the length of a buffer required to hold the data elements in the list.

You can use this function to improve the example just shown by using **epos** to compute the size of the extracted record:

```
static int rlist[]={PROJECT_NAME, AMT_EXPENDED, 0};
char *rcd, malloc();
struct projects pr;
    .
rcd = malloc(epos(0, rlist));
    .
rcd_fill(&pr, rcd, file_ele[PROJECTS], rlist);
    .
```

The **epos** function returns the length required for a buffer that can contain a record as described by the data element list named **rlist**. You can use the function as the parameter for the standard C memory allocation function, **malloc**. When you have changed the list or a data element length, modification of the buffer length is unnecessary. In the earlier example, **rcd** is a character array whose length must match that of the extracted record format. In this example, **rcd** is a character pointer that points to a space equal in length to the computed length of the extracted record.

Function rlen:

```
int rlen(f)
int f;          /* file number */
```

The **rlen** function returns the length of the data base record for the file specified in the parameter. Use this function wherever you need to allocate a buffer or if you use **mov_mem** to move a buffer where the buffer length is not known at compile time (for example, by use of the **sizeof** operator).

Function init_rcd:

```
init_rcd(f, bf)
int f;          /* file number */
char *bf;       /* buffer */
```

Use this function when you want to initialize a data base file's record buffer to null values. It sets each data element field in the buffer to a null-terminated string of spaces.

Function clrrcd:

```
clrrcd(bf, els)
char *bf;    /* buffer */
int *els;    /* data element list */
```

Clrrcd is similar to **init_rcd** in that it sets a buffer to null-terminated strings of spaces. But **clrrcd** has more general application. Rather than operating on data base file records as defined in the schema, **clrrcd** will initialize a buffer by using the data element list you pass to it. This permits you to construct working buffers made up of data elements where the format of the buffer does not necessarily conform to the format of one of the files.

CDATA SOURCE LISTINGS

The Cdata DDL and DML are now complete. You have the tools necessary to design, define, and build a relational data base. Immediately following are Listings 6.13 through 6.17. These listings contain the source code for the Cdata DML functions and supporting software. The functions of the DML are included along with several low-level file and index management functions. These functions, when linked with your code, represent the Cheap Data Base Management System (Cdata).

To complete the package, Chapter 7 presents a set of utility functions and programs that support the Cdata data base environment. These programs include initialization utilities, a query and data entry program, a general purpose report program, and a program to regenerate index files from data already in a data file.

Data Base Manager (database.c)

Database.c (Listing 6.13) is the source file containing the functions described in this chapter that your applications programs will use for data base storage and retrievals. It also contains the utility functions described above. Besides the functions already described, **database.c** includes several index management functions that are called from within the data base functions to manage the maintenance and retrieval of index key values in the B-tree index files. These index managers react to the schema key specifications whenever records are to be retrieved, stored, or deleted by the data base management functions.

Listing 6.13 (database.c)

```
/* ---------------- database.c --------------------- */

#include <stdio.h>
#include "cdata.h"
#include "keys.h"

void build_b();          /* Builds a new B-tree              */
RPTR locate();           /* Searches a B-tree for a key      */
RPTR nextkey();          /* Gets address of the next key     */
RPTR prevkey();          /* Gets address of the previous key */
RPTR firstkey();         /* Gets address of first key        */
RPTR lastkey();          /* Gets address of last key         */
RPTR currkey();          /* Gets address of current key      */
void file_close();       /* Closes a data file              */
RPTR new_record();       /* Adds a record to a file          */
char *malloc();
void init_index(), cls_index(), del_indexes();

int db_opened = FALSE;   /* data base opened indicator       */
int curr_fd [MXFILS];    /* current file descriptor          */
RPTR curr_a [MXFILS];    /* current record file address      */
char *bfs [MXFILS];      /* file i/o buffers */
int bfd [MXFILS] [MXINDEX];
char dbpath [64];
int notice_posted = 0;
int prev_col = 0, prev_row = 0;

/* ------------------ open the data base ---------------- */
void db_open(path, fl)
char *path;
int *fl;
{
    char fnm [64];
    int i;

    if (!db_opened) {
        for (i = 0; i < MXFILS; i++)
            curr_fd [i] = -1;
        db_opened = TRUE;
    }
```

continued...

...from previous page

```
    strcpy(dbpath, path);
    while (*fl != -1)    {
        sprintf(fnm, "%s%.8s.dat", path, dbfiles [*fl]);
        curr_fd [*fl] = file_open(fnm);
        init_index(path, *fl);
        if ((bfs [*fl] = malloc(rlen(*fl))) == NULL)     {
            errno = D_OM;
            dberror();
        }
        fl++;
    }
}


/* ------------- add a record to a file -------------- */
int add_rcd(f, bf)
int f;
char *bf;
{
    RPTR ad;
    extern RPTR new_record();
    int rtn;

    if ((rtn = relate_rcd(f, bf)) != ERROR) {
        ad = new_record(curr_fd [f], bf);
        if ((rtn = add_indexes(f, bf, ad)) == ERROR)     {
            errno = D_DUPL;
            delete_record(curr_fd [f], ad);
        }
    }
    return rtn;
}


/* ------------- find a record in a file ------------- */
int find_rcd(f,k,key,bf)
int f;              /* file number            */
int k;              /* key number             */
char *key;          /* key value              */
char *bf;           /* buffer for record      */
{
    RPTR ad;
```

continued...

...from previous page

```
    if ((ad = locate(treeno(f,k), key)) == 0)   {
        errno = D_NF;
        return ERROR;
    }
    return getrcd(f, ad, bf);
}

/* -------- verify that a record is in a file --------- */
int verify_rcd(f,k,key)
int f;          /* file number           */
int k;          /* key number            */
char *key;      /* key value             */
{
    if (locate(treeno(f,k), key) == (RPTR) 0)   {
        errno = D_NF;
        return ERROR;
    }
    return OK;
}

/* ------- find the first indexed record in a file -------- */
int first_rcd(f,k,bf)
int f;          /* file number           */
int k;          /* key number            */
char *bf;       /* buffer for record     */
{
    RPTR ad;

    if ((ad = firstkey(treeno(f,k))) == 0)  {
        errno = D_EOF;
        return ERROR;
    }
    return getrcd(f, ad, bf);
}

/* ------- find the last indexed record in a file -------- */
int last_rcd(f,k,bf)
int f;          /* file number           */
int k;          /* key number            */
```

continued...

...from previous page

```
char *bf;          /* buffer for record    */
{
    RPTR ad;

    if ((ad = lastkey(treeno(f,k))) == 0)    {
        errno = D_BOF;
        return ERROR;
    }
    return getrcd(f, ad, bf);
}

/* ------------- find the next record in a file ----------- */
int next_rcd(f,k,bf)
int f;             /* file number          */
int k;             /* key number           */
char *bf;          /* buffer for record    */
{
    RPTR ad;

    if ((ad = nextkey(treeno(f, k))) == 0)  {
        errno = D_EOF;
        return ERROR;
    }
    return getrcd(f, ad, bf);
}

/* -------- find the previous record in a file --------- */
int prev_rcd(f,k,bf)
int f;             /* file number          */
int k;             /* key number           */
char *bf;          /* buffer for record    */
{
    RPTR ad;

    if ((ad = prevkey(treeno(f,k))) == 0)    {
        errno = D_BOF;
        return ERROR;
    }
    return getrcd(f, ad, bf);
}
```

continued...

...from previous page

```
/* ----- return the current record to the data base ------- */
int rtn_rcd(f, bf)
int f;
char *bf;
{
    int rtn;

    if (curr_a [f] == 0)    {
        errno = D_PRIOR;
        return ERROR;
    }
    if ((rtn = relate_rcd(f, bf)) != ERROR) {
        del_indexes(f, curr_a [f]);
        if ((rtn = add_indexes(f, bf, curr_a [f])) == OK)
            put_record(curr_fd [f], curr_a [f], bf);
        else
            errno = D_DUPL;
    }
    return rtn;
}


/* ------- delete the current record from the file -------- */
int del_rcd(f)
int f;
{
    if (curr_a [f]) {
        del_indexes(f, curr_a [f]);
        delete_record(curr_fd [f], curr_a [f]);
        curr_a [f] = 0;
        return OK;
    }
    errno = D_PRIOR;
    return ERROR;
}
```

continued...

...from previous page

```
/* ---------- find the current record in a file ----------- */
int curr_rcd(f,k,bf)
int f;          /* file number          */
int k;          /* key number           */
char *bf;       /* buffer for record    */
{
    RPTR ad;
    extern RPTR currkey();

    if ((ad = currkey(treeno(f,k))) == 0)   {
        errno = D_NF;
        return ERROR;
    }
    getrcd(f, ad, bf);
    return OK;
}

/* --------- get the next physical
                  sequential record from the file ------- */
int seqrcd(f, bf)
int f;
RPTR *bf;
{
    RPTR ad;
    int rtn;

    do  {
        ad = ++curr_a [f];
        if ((rtn = (rel_rcd(f,ad,bf)))==ERROR && errno!=D_NF)
            break;
    }   while (errno == D_NF);
    return rtn;
}

/* ----------------- close the data base ------------------ */
void db_cls()
{
    int f;

    for (f = 0; f < MXFILS; f++)
```

continued...

...from previous page

```
        if (curr_fd [f] != -1)  {
            file_close(curr_fd [f]);
            cls_index(f);
            free(bfs[f]);
            curr_fd [f] = -1;
        }
    db_opened = FALSE;
}

/* ------------------- data base error routine ----------- */
void dberror()
{
    static char *ers [] = {
        "Record not found",
        "No prior record",
        "End of file",
        "Beginning of file",
        "Record already exists",
        "Not enough memory",
        "Index corrupted",
        "Disk i/o error"
    };
    static int fat [] = {0,1,0,0,0,1,1,1};

    error_message(ers [errno-1]);
    if (fat [errno-1])
        exit(1);
}

/* ----------- compute file record length ---------------- */
int rlen(f)
int f;
{
    return epos(0, file_ele [f]);
}
```

continued...

...from previous page

```
/* ---------- initialize a file record buffer ------------ */
void init_rcd(f, bf)
int f;          /* file number */
char *bf;       /* buffer */
{
    clrrcd(bf, file_ele[f]);
}

/* -------- set a generic record buffer to blanks --------- */
void clrrcd(bf, els)
char *bf;       /* buffer */
int *els;       /* data element list */
{
    int ln, i = 0, el;
    char *rb;

    while (*(els + i))  {
        el = *(els + i);
        rb = bf + epos(el, els);
        ln = ellen [el - 1];
        while (ln--)
            *rb++ = ' ';
        *rb = '\0';
        i++;
    }
}


/* ------- move data from one record to another ------- */
void rcd_fill(s, d, slist, dlist)
char *s;        /* source record buffer */
char *d;        /* destination record buffer */
int *slist;     /* source data element list */
int *dlist;     /* destination data element list */
{
    int *s1, *d1;

    s1 = slist;
    while (*s1) {
        d1 = dlist;
```

continued...

...from previous page

```
        while (*d1) {
            if (*s1 == *d1)
                strcpy(d+epos(*d1,dlist), s+epos(*s1,slist));
            d1++;
        }
        s1++;
    }
}


/* -------- compute relative position of
                a data element within a record -----*/
int epos(el, list)
int el;         /* element number */
int *list;      /* record element list */
{
    int len = 0;

    while (el != *list)
        len += ellen [(*list++)-1] + 1;
    return len;
}


/* ------------- index management functions ------------ */
/* ---- initialize the indices for a file ---- */
static void init_index(path, f)
char *path;     /* where the data base is */
int f;          /* file number */
{
    char xname [64];
    int x = 0;

    while (*(index_ele [f] + x))     {
        sprintf(xname, "%s%.8s.x%02d",path,dbfiles[f],x+1);
        if ((bfd [f] [x++] = btree_init(xname)) == ERROR)   {
            printf("\n%s", xname);
            errno = D_INDXC;
            dberror();
        }
    }
}
```

continued...

...from previous page

```
/* ---- build the indices for a file ---- */
void build_index(path, f)
char *path;
int f;            /* file number */
{
    char xname [64];
    int x = 0, x1;
    int len;

    while (*(index_ele [f] + x))      {
        sprintf(xname, "%s%.8s.x%02d", path, dbfiles[f], x+1);
        len = 0;
        x1 = 0;
        while (*(*(index_ele [f] + x) + x1))
            len += ellen [*(*(index_ele [f] + x) + (x1++))-1];
        build_b(xname, len);
        x++;
    }
}

/* ----- close the indices for a file ------ */
static void cls_index(f)
int f;
{
    int x = 0;

    while (*(index_ele [f] + x))      {
        if (bfd [f] [x] != ERROR)
            btree_close(bfd [f] [x]);
        x++;
    }
}
```

continued...

...from previous page

```
/* ---- add index values from a record to the indices ---- */
int add_indexes(f, bf, ad)
int f;
char *bf;
RPTR ad;
{
    int x = 0;
    int i;
    char key [MXKEYLEN];

    while (*(index_ele [f] + x))     {
        *key = '\0';
        i = 0;
        while(*(*(index_ele [f] + x) + i))
            strcat(key,
                bf +
            epos(*(*(index_ele[f]+x)+(i++)),file_ele [f]));
        if (insertkey(bfd [f] [x], key, ad, !x) == ERROR)
            return ERROR;
        x++;
    }
    return OK;
}

/* --- delete index values in a record from the indices --- */
static void del_indexes(f, ad)
int f;
RPTR ad;
{
    char *bf;
    int x = 0;
    int i;
    char key [MXKEYLEN];

    if ((bf = malloc(rlen(f))) == NULL) {
        errno = D_OM;
        dberror();
    }
    get_record(curr_fd [f], ad, bf);
    while (*(index_ele [f] + x))     {
```

continued...

...from previous page

```
        *key = '\0';
        i = 0;
        while (*(*(index_ele [f] + x) + i))
            strcat(key,
                bf +
            epos(*(*(index_ele[f]+x)+(i++)), file_ele [f]));
        deletekey(bfd [f] [x++], key, ad);
    }
    free(bf);
}



/* ---- compute tree number from file and key number ---- */
static int treeno(f, k)
int f, k;
{
    return bfd [f] [k - 1];
}



/* ---- validate the contents of a record where its file is
        related to another file in the data base ---------- */
static int relate_rcd(f, bf)
int f;
char *bf;
{
    int fx = 0, mx, *fp;
    static int ff[] = {0, -1};
    char *cp;

    while (dbfiles [fx])    {
        if (fx != f && *(*(index_ele [fx]) + 1) == 0)    {
            mx = *(*(index_ele [fx]));
            fp = file_ele [f];
            while (*fp) {
                if (*fp == mx)   {
                    cp = bf + epos(mx, file_ele [f]);
                    if (data_in(cp))    {
                        if (curr_fd[fx] == -1)   {
                            *ff = fx;
```

continued...

...from previous page

```
                                db_open(dbpath, ff);
                    }
                    if (verify_rcd(fx, 1, cp) == ERROR)
                        return ERROR;
                }
                break;
            }
            fp++;
        }
        }
        fx++;
    }
    return OK;
}

/* ----- test a string for data. return TRUE if any ---- */
static int data_in(c)
char *c;
{
    while (*c == ' ')
        c++;
    return (*c != '\0');
}

/* ------------- get a record from a file ------------- */
static int getrcd(f, ad, bf)
int f;
RPTR ad;
char *bf;
{
    get_record(curr_fd [f], ad, bf);
    curr_a [f] = ad;
    return OK;
}

extern FHEADER fh [];
```

continued...

...from previous page

```
/* ----- find a record by relative record number ------ */
static int rel_rcd(f, ad, bf)
int f;              /* file number           */
RPTR ad;
int *bf;
{
    errno = 0;
    if (ad >= fh [curr_fd [f]].next_record) {
        errno = D_EOF;
        return ERROR;
    }
    getrcd(f, ad, bf);
    if (*bf == -1)  {
        errno = D_NF;
        return ERROR;
    }
    return OK;
}

/* -------------- error message -------- */
void error_message(s)
char *s;
{
    put_char(BELL);
    post_notice(s);
}

/* --------- clear notice line ------------- */
void clear_notice()
{
    int i;

    if (notice_posted)  {
        cursor(0,24);
        for (i = 0; i < 50; i++)
            put_char(' ');
        notice_posted = FALSE;
        cursor(prev_col, prev_row);
    }
}
```

continued...

...from previous page

```
/* ---------- post a notice ---------------- */
void post_notice(s)
char *s;
{
    clear_notice();
    cursor(0,24);
    while (*s)  {
        put_char(isprint(*s) ? *s : '.');
        s++;
    }
    cursor(prev_col, prev_row);
    notice_posted = TRUE;
}

/* ---------- Move a block -------- */
void mov_mem(s, d, l)
char *s, *d;
int l;
{
    if (d > s)
        while (l--)
            *(d + l) = *(s + l);
    else
        while (l--)
            *d++ = *s++;
}

/* --------- Set a block to a character value ----- */
void set_mem(s, l, n)
char *s, n;
int l;
{
    while (l--)
        *s++ = n;
}
```

continued...

...from previous page

```c
/*
 * Convert a file name into its file token.
 * Return the token,
 * or ERROR if the file name is not in the schema.
 */
int filename(fn)
char *fn;
{
    char fname[32];
    int f;
    void name_cvt();

    name_cvt(fname, fn);
    for (f = 0; dbfiles [f]; f++)
        if (strcmp(fname, dbfiles [f]) == 0)
            break;
    if (dbfiles [f] == 0)   {
        fprintf(stderr, "\nNo such file as %s", fname);
        return ERROR;
    }
    return f;
}

/* ----------- convert a name to upper case ---------- */
void name_cvt(c2, c1)
char *c1, *c2;
{
    while (*c1) {
        *c2 = toupper(*c1);
        c1++;
        c2++;
    }
    *c2 = '\0';
}
```

Refer back to the diagram in Figure 6.4. **Database.c** is in the symbol that is labeled "Data Base Management Software."

File Manager (datafile.c)

Datafile.c (Listing 6.14) is the source file that contains the data file management functions for the data base manager. It includes functions to create data files and to add, change, and delete records in data files.

(Listing 6.14 on next page)

Listing 6.14 (datafile.c)

```c
/* --------------- datafile.c ------------------------ */

#include <stdio.h>
#include "cdata.h"

#define flocate(r,l) ((long)(sizeof(FHEADER)+(((r)-1)*(l))))

static int handle [MXFILS];
FHEADER fh [MXFILS];

/* --------- create a file ----------- */
void file_create(name, len)
char *name;
int len;
{
    int fp;
    FHEADER hd;
#if COMPILER == MICROSOFT
    extern int _iomode;
    _iomode = 0x8000;
#endif
#if COMPILER == LATTICE
    extern int _iomode;
    _iomode = 0x8000;
#endif

    unlink(name);
    fp = creat(name, CMODE);
    close(fp);
    fp = open(name, OPENMODE);
    hd.next_record = 1;
    hd.first_record = 0;
    hd.record_length = len;
    write(fp, (char *) &hd, sizeof hd);
    close(fp);
}
```

continued...

...from previous page

```
/* -------------- open a file ---------------- */
int file_open(name)
char *name;
{
    int fp;
#if COMPILER == MICROSOFT
    extern int _iomode;
    _iomode = 0x8000;
#endif
#if COMPILER == LATTICE
    extern int _iomode;
    _iomode = 0x8000;
#endif

    for (fp = 0; fp < MXFILS; fp++)
        if (handle [fp] == 0)
            break;
    if (fp == MXFILS)
        return ERROR;
    if ((handle [fp] = open(name, OPENMODE)) == ERROR)
        return ERROR;
    lseek(handle [fp], 0L, 0);
    read(handle [fp], (char *) &fh [fp], sizeof(FHEADER));
    return fp;
}

/* -------------- close a file ---------------- */
void file_close(fp)
int fp;
{
    lseek(handle [fp], 0L, 0);
    write(handle [fp], (char *) &fh [fp], sizeof(FHEADER));
    close(handle [fp]);
    handle [fp] = 0;
}
```

continued...

...from previous page

```
/* -------------- create a new record ------------- */
RPTR new_record(fp, bf)
int fp;
char *bf;
{
    RPTR rcdno;
    extern char *malloc();
    FHEADER *c;
    extern int free();

    if (fh [fp].first_record)   {
        rcdno = fh [fp].first_record;
        if ((c = (FHEADER *)
                malloc(fh [fp].record_length)) == NULL) {
            errno = D_OM;
            dberror();
        }
        get_record(fp, rcdno, c);
        fh [fp].first_record = c->next_record;
        free(c);
    }
    else
        rcdno = fh [fp].next_record++;
    put_record(fp, rcdno, bf);
    return rcdno;
}

/* --------------- retrieve a record -------------- */
int get_record(fp, rcdno, bf)
int fp;
RPTR rcdno;
char *bf;
{
    if (rcdno >= fh [fp].next_record)
        return ERROR;
    lseek(handle [fp],
            flocate(rcdno, fh [fp].record_length), 0);
    read(handle [fp], bf, fh [fp].record_length);
    return OK;
}
```

continued...

...from previous page

```
/* ---------------- rewrite a record ------------- */
int put_record(fp, rcdno, bf)
int fp;
RPTR rcdno;
char *bf;
{
    if (rcdno > fh [fp].next_record)
        return ERROR;
    lseek(handle [fp],
                flocate(rcdno, fh [fp].record_length), 0);
    write(handle [fp], bf, fh [fp].record_length);
    return OK;
}


/* -------------- delete a record --------------- */
int delete_record(fp, rcdno)
int fp;
RPTR rcdno;
{
    FHEADER *bf;
    extern char *malloc();

    if (rcdno > fh [fp].next_record)
        return ERROR;
    if ((bf = (FHEADER *)
            malloc(fh [fp].record_length)) == NULL) {
        errno = D_OM;
        dberror();
    }
    set_mem(bf, fh [fp].record_length, '\0');
    bf->next_record = fh [fp].first_record;
    bf->first_record = -1;
    fh [fp].first_record = rcdno;
    put_record(fp, rcdno, bf);
    free(bf);
    return OK;
}
```

Refer back to the diagram in Figure 6.4. **Datafile.c** is in the symbol that is labeled "Data File Software."

You might never have a reason to use the functions in **datafile.c**, but they are described here so that you can better understand your system.

Function file_create:

```
void file_create(name, len)
char *name;
int len;
```

This function is used to create a data file and is called from **dbinit.c** when the files for the data base are initialized. The **name** pointer points to the DOS file name of the data file. The **len** integer is the file's record length.

Function file_open:

```
int file_open(name)
char *name;
```

This function opens an existing data file, one that was previously created by **file_create**, and returns a "file pointer" that is used for subsequent calls to data file functions. If the file does not exist, ERROR is returned.

Function file_close:

```
void file_close(fp)
int fp;
```

This function closes a data file.

Function new_record:

```
RPTR new_record(fp, bf)
int fp;
char *bf;
```

This function is used to add a record to a data file. Records are added to the next available record space in the file, either at the end of the file or into a record position that was released when another record was deleted.

The **RPTR** return value is a typedef in **cdata.h**. It will be either an integer or a long integer, and it will represent the logical record position within the file that was assigned to the record. The **RPTR** value is relative to one.

Function get_record:

```
int get_record(fp, rcdno, bf)
int fp;
RPTR rcdno;
char *bf;
```

This function retrieves a record that was previously stored in the data file. The **RPTR rcdno** parameter is the logical record number where the record is known to be stored. The **bf** pointer points to the buffer where the record will be copied when it is read from disk.

Function put_record:

```
int put_record(fp, rcdno, bf)
int fp;
RPTR rcdno;
char *bf;
```

This function is called to rewrite a record to the file and is used when the record has been changed. The parameters are the same as for **get__record**.

Function delete_record:

```
int delete_record(fp, rcdno)
int fp;
RPTR rcdno;
```

This function deletes the record located at logical record position **rcdno**. The record space is placed into a linked list for the file so that a later record addition can reuse the space.

Index Manager (btree.c)

Listing 6.15 is the source file **btree.c**. This group of functions manages the data base B-tree index files. The functions are generic B-tree managers, and the index management functions in **database.c** use them. They include functions to create and search B-trees, add and delete keys in B-trees, and navigate B-trees in ascending or descending key sequence. The key entries in the B-tree files yield data file record addresses that point to the data file records that match the key values. As such, the B-tree mechanism supports multiple inverted indexes into the relational data base flat files.

Listing 6.15 (btree.c)

```c
/* -------------------- btree.c ---------------------- */
#include <stdio.h>
#include "cdata.h"

#define MXTREES 20
#define ADR sizeof(RPTR)
#define KLEN bheader[trx].keylength
#define ENTLN (KLEN+ADR)

/* --------- the btree node structure ------------- */
typedef struct treenode {
    int nonleaf;      /* 0 if leaf, 1 if non-leaf           */
    RPTR prntnode;    /* parent node                        */
    RPTR lfsib;       /* left sibling node                  */
    RPTR rtsib;       /* right sibling node                 */
    int keyct;        /* number of keys                     */
    RPTR key0;        /* node # of keys < 1st key this node */
    char keyspace [NODE - ((sizeof(int) * 2) + (ADR * 4))];
    char spil [MXKEYLEN];  /* for insertion excess */
} BTREE;

/* ---- the structure of the btree header node --------- */
typedef struct treehdr  {
    RPTR rootnode;           /* root node number */
    int keylength;
    int m;                   /* max keys/node  */
    RPTR rlsed_node;         /* next released node */
    RPTR endnode;            /* next unassigned node  */
    int locked;              /* if btree is locked  */
    RPTR leftmost;           /* left-most node */
    RPTR rightmost;          /* right-most node */
} HEADER;

HEADER bheader [MXTREES];
BTREE trnode;

int handle     [MXTREES];  /* handle of each index in use */
RPTR currnode  [MXTREES];  /* node number of current key  */
int currkno    [MXTREES];  /* key number of current key   */
int trx;                   /* current tree */
```

continued...

...from previous page

```
char *malloc(), *childptr();
void redist(),adopt(),implode(),
    read_node(),write_node(),bseek();
RPTR firstkey(),lastkey(),scannext(),scanprev(),
    leaflevel(),nextnode(),fileaddr();

/* -------- initiate b-tree processing ---------- */
int btree_init(ndx_name)
char *ndx_name;
{
#if COMPILER == MICROSOFT
    extern int _iomode;
    _iomode = 0x8000;
#endif
#if COMPILER == LATTICE
    extern int _iomode;
    _iomode = 0x8000;
#endif
    for (trx = 0; trx < MXTREES; trx++)
        if (handle [trx] == 0)
            break;
    if (trx == MXTREES)
        return ERROR;
    if ((handle [trx] = open(ndx_name, OPENMODE)) == ERROR)
        return ERROR;
    lseek(handle [trx], 0L, 0);
    read(handle [trx],(char *) &bheader[trx],sizeof(HEADER));
    if (bheader[trx].locked)    {
        close(handle [trx]);
        handle [trx] = 0;
        return ERROR;
    }
    bheader[trx].locked = TRUE;
    lseek(handle [trx], 0L, 0);
    write(handle [trx],(char *) &bheader[trx],sizeof(HEADER));
    currnode [trx] = 0;
    currkno [trx] = 0;
    return trx;
}
```

continued...

...from previous page

```
/* ----------- terminate b tree processing ------------ */
int btree_close(tree)
int tree;
{
    if (tree >= MXTREES || handle [tree] == 0)
        return ERROR;
    bheader[tree].locked = FALSE;
    lseek(handle[tree], 0L, 0);
    write(handle[tree],(char *)&bheader[tree],sizeof(HEADER));
    close(handle[tree]);
    handle[tree] = 0;
    return OK;
}


/* --------Build a new .b-tree ----------------- */
void build_b(name, len)
char *name;
int len;
{
    HEADER *bhdp;
    int fd;
#if COMPILER == MICROSOFT
    extern int _iomode;
    _iomode = 0x8000;
#endif
#if COMPILER == LATTICE
    extern int _iomode;
    _iomode = 0x8000;
#endif

    if ((bhdp = (HEADER *)malloc(NODE))==(HEADER *)NULL)    {
        errno = D_OM;
        dberror();
    }
    set_mem(bhdp, NODE, '\0');
    bhdp->keylength = len;
    bhdp->m = ((NODE-((sizeof(int)*2)+(ADR*4)))/(len+ADR));
    bhdp->endnode = 1;
    unlink(name);
    fd = creat(name, CMODE);
```

continued...

...from previous page

```
    close(fd);
    fd = open(name, OPENMODE);
    write(fd, (char *) bhdp, NODE);
    close(fd);
    free(bhdp);
}

/* --------------- Locate key in the b-tree -------------- */
RPTR locate(tree, k)
int tree;
char *k;
{
    int i, fnd = FALSE;
    RPTR t, ad;
    char *a;

    trx = tree;
    t = bheader[trx].rootnode;
    if (t)  {
        read_node(t, &trnode);
        fnd = btreescan(&t, k, &a);
        ad = leaflevel(&t, &a, &i);
        if (i == trnode.keyct + 1)  {
            i = 0;
            t = trnode.rtsib;
        }
        currnode [trx] = t;
        currkno [trx] = i;
    }
    return fnd ? ad : (RPTR) 0;
}

/* ----------- Search tree ------------- */
static int btreescan(t, k, a)
RPTR *t;
char *k, **a;
{
    int nl;
    do {
        if (nodescan(k, a)) {
```

continued...

...from previous page

```
            while (compare_keys(*a, k) == FALSE)
                if (scanprev(t, a) == 0)
                    break;
            if (compare_keys(*a, k))
                scannext(t, a);
            return TRUE;
        }
        nl = trnode.nonleaf;
        if (nl) {
            *t = *((RPTR *) (*a - ADR));
            read_node(*t, &trnode);
        }
    }   while (nl);
    return FALSE;
}

/* ----------------- Search node ------------ */
static int nodescan(keyvalue, nodeadr)
char *keyvalue, **nodeadr;
{
    int i;
    int result;

    *nodeadr = trnode.keyspace;
    for (i = 0; i < trnode.keyct; i++)  {
        result = compare_keys(keyvalue, *nodeadr);
        if (result == FALSE) return TRUE;
        if (result < 0) return FALSE;
        *nodeadr += ENTLN;
    }
    return FALSE;
}

/* ------------- Compare keys ----------- */
static int compare_keys(a, b)
char *a, *b;
{
    int len = KLEN, cm;

    while (len--)
```

continued...

...from previous page

```
        if ((cm = (int) *a++ - (int) *b++) != 0)
            break;
    return cm;
}


/* ------------ Compute current file address  ------------ */
static RPTR fileaddr(t, a)
RPTR t;
char *a;
{
    RPTR cn, ti;
    int i;

    ti = t;
    cn = leaflevel(&ti, &a, &i);
    read_node(t, &trnode);
    return cn;
}


/* ---------------- Navigate down to leaf level ------------ */
static RPTR leaflevel(t, a, p)
RPTR *t;
char **a;
int *p;
{
    if (trnode.nonleaf == FALSE)    { /* already at a leaf? */
        *p = (*a - trnode.keyspace) / ENTLN + 1;
        return *((RPTR *) (*a + KLEN));
    }
    *p = 0;
    *t = *((RPTR *) (*a + KLEN));
    read_node(*t, &trnode);
    *a = trnode.keyspace;
    while (trnode.nonleaf)  {
        *t = trnode.key0;
        read_node(*t, &trnode);
    }
    return trnode.key0;
}
```

continued...

...from previous page

```
/* -------------- Delete a key  ------------- */
int deletekey(tree, x, ad)
int tree;
char *x;
RPTR ad;
{
    BTREE *qp, *yp;
    int rt_len, comb;
    RPTR p, adr, q, *b, y, z;
    char *a;

    trx = tree;
    if (trx >= MXTREES || handle [trx] == 0)
        return ERROR;
    p = bheader[trx].rootnode;
    if (p == 0)
        return OK;
    read_node(p, &trnode);
    if (btreescan(&p, x, &a) == FALSE)
        return OK;
    adr = fileaddr(p, a);
    while (adr != ad)    {
        adr = scannext(&p, &a);
        if (compare_keys(a, x))
            return OK;
    }
    if (trnode.nonleaf) {
        b = (RPTR *) (a + KLEN);
        q = *b;
        if ((qp=(BTREE *) malloc(NODE))==(BTREE *) NULL)    {
            errno = D_OM;
            dberror();
        }
        read_node(q, qp);
        while (qp->nonleaf) {
            q = qp->key0;
            read_node(q, qp);
        }
    /* Move the left-most key from the leaf
                        to where the deleted key is */
```

continued...

...from previous page

```
        mov_mem(qp->keyspace, a, KLEN);
        write_node(p, &trnode);
        p = q;
        mov_mem(qp, &trnode, sizeof trnode);
        a = trnode.keyspace;
        b = (RPTR *) (a + KLEN);
        trnode.key0 = *b;
        free(qp);
    }
    currnode [trx] = p;
    currkno [trx] = (a - trnode.keyspace) / ENTLN;
    rt_len = (trnode.keyspace + (bheader[trx].m * ENTLN)) - a;
    mov_mem(a + ENTLN, a, rt_len);
    set_mem(a + rt_len, ENTLN, '\0');
    trnode.keyct--;
    if (currkno [trx] > trnode.keyct)    {
        if (trnode.rtsib)    {
            currnode [trx] = trnode.rtsib;
            currkno [trx] = 0;
        }
        else
            currkno [trx]--;
    }
    while (trnode.keyct <= bheader[trx].m / 2 &&
                            p != bheader[trx].rootnode) {
        comb = FALSE;
        z = trnode.prntnode;
        if ((yp=(BTREE *) malloc(NODE))==(BTREE *) NULL)    {
            errno = D_OM;
            dberror();
        }
        if (trnode.rtsib)    {
            y = trnode.rtsib;
            read_node(y, yp);
            if (yp->keyct + trnode.keyct <
                    bheader[trx].m && yp->prntnode == z)    {
                comb = TRUE;
                implode(&trnode, yp);
            }
        }
```

continued...

...from previous page

```
        if (comb == FALSE && trnode.lfsib)  {
            y = trnode.lfsib;
            read_node(y, yp);
            if (yp->prntnode == z)  {
                if (yp->keyct + trnode.keyct <
                                    bheader[trx].m) {
                    comb = TRUE;
                    implode(yp, &trnode);
                }
                else    {
                    redist(yp, &trnode);
                    write_node(p, &trnode);
                    write_node(y, yp);
                    free(yp);
                    return OK;
                }
            }
        }
        if (comb == FALSE)  {
            y = trnode.rtsib;
            read_node(y, yp);
            redist(&trnode, yp);
            write_node(y, yp);
            write_node(p, &trnode);
            free(yp);
            return OK;
        }
        free(yp);
        p = z;
        read_node(p, &trnode);
    }
    if (trnode.keyct == 0)  {
        bheader[trx].rootnode = trnode.key0;
        trnode.nonleaf = FALSE;
        trnode.key0 = 0;
        trnode.prntnode = bheader[trx].rlsed_node;
        bheader[trx].rlsed_node = p;
    }
    if (bheader[trx].rootnode == 0)
        bheader[trx].rightmost = bheader[trx].leftmost = 0;
```

continued...

...from previous page

```
    write_node(p, &trnode);
    return OK;
}

/* ------------ Combine two sibling nodes. ------------ */
static void implode(left, right)
BTREE *left, *right;
{
    RPTR lf, rt, p;
    int rt_len, lf_len;
    char *a;
    RPTR *b;
    BTREE *par;
    RPTR c;
    char *j;

    lf = right->lfsib;
    rt = left->rtsib;
    p = left->prntnode;
    if ((par = (BTREE *) malloc(NODE)) == (BTREE *) NULL)   {
        errno = D_OM;
        dberror();
    }
    j = childptr(lf, p, par);
/* --- move key from parent to end of left sibling --- */
    lf_len = left->keyct * ENTLN;
    a = left->keyspace + lf_len;
    mov_mem(j, a, KLEN);
    set_mem(j, ENTLN, '\0');
/* --- move keys from right sibling to left --- */
    b = (RPTR *) (a + KLEN);
    *b = right->key0;
    rt_len = right->keyct * ENTLN;
    a = (char *) (b + 1);
    mov_mem(right->keyspace, a, rt_len);
/* --- point lower nodes to their new parent --- */
    if (left->nonleaf)
        adopt(b, right->keyct + 1, lf);
/* --- if global key pointers -> to the right sibling,
                                change to -> left --- */
```

continued...

...from previous page

```
    if (currnode [trx] == left->rtsib)  {
        currnode [trx] = right->lfsib;
        currkno [trx] += left->keyct + 1;
    }
/* --- update control values in left sibling node --- */
    left->keyct += right->keyct + 1;
    c = bheader[trx].rlsed_node;
    bheader[trx].rlsed_node = left->rtsib;
    if (bheader[trx].rightmost == left->rtsib)
        bheader[trx].rightmost = right->lfsib;
    left->rtsib = right->rtsib;
/* --- point the deleted node's right brother
                            to this left brother --- */
    if (left->rtsib)    {
        read_node(left->rtsib, right);
        right->lfsib = lf;
        write_node(left->rtsib, right);
    }
    set_mem(right, NODE, '\0');
    right->prntnode = c;
/* --- remove key from parent node --- */
    par->keyct--;
    if (par->keyct == 0)
        left->prntnode = 0;
    else    {
        rt_len = par->keyspace + (par->keyct * ENTLN) - j;
        mov_mem(j + ENTLN, j, rt_len);
    }
    write_node(lf, left);
    write_node(rt, right);
    write_node(p, par);
    free(par);
}
```

continued...

...from previous page

```
/* ----------------- Insert key ------------------- */
int insertkey(tree, x, ad, unique)
int tree;
char *x;
RPTR ad;
int unique;
{
    char k [MXKEYLEN + 1], *a;
    BTREE *yp;
    BTREE *bp;
    int nl_flag, rt_len, j;
    RPTR t, p, sv;
    RPTR *b;
    int lshft, rshft;

    trx = tree;
    if (trx >= MXTREES || handle [trx] == 0)
        return ERROR;
    p = 0;
    sv = 0;
    nl_flag = 0;
    mov_mem(x, k, KLEN);
    t = bheader[trx].rootnode;
    /* -------------- Find insertion point ------- */
    if (t) {
        read_node(t, &trnode);
        if (btreescan(&t, k, &a))   {
            if (unique)
                return ERROR;
            else   {
                leaflevel(&t, &a, &j);
                currkno [trx] = j;
            }
        }
        else
            currkno [trx] = ((a - trnode.keyspace) / ENTLN)+1;
        currnode [trx] = t;
    }
    /* --------- Insert key into leaf node -------------- */
    while (t)   {
```

continued...

...from previous page

```
nl_flag = 1;
rt_len = (trnode.keyspace+(bheader[trx].m*ENTLN))-a;
mov_mem(a, a + ENTLN, rt_len);
mov_mem(k, a, KLEN);
b = (RPTR *) (a + KLEN);
*b = ad;
if (trnode.nonleaf == FALSE)     {
    currnode [trx] = t;
    currkno [trx] = ((a - trnode.keyspace) / ENTLN)+1;
}
trnode.keyct++;
if (trnode.keyct <= bheader[trx].m) {
    write_node(t, &trnode);
    return OK;
}
/* --- Redistribute keys between sibling nodes ---*/
lshft = FALSE;
rshft = FALSE;
if ((yp=(BTREE *) malloc(NODE))==(BTREE *) NULL)     {
    errno = D_OM;
    dberror();
}
if (trnode.lfsib)     {
    read_node(trnode.lfsib, yp);
    if (yp->keyct < bheader[trx].m &&
                yp->prntnode == trnode.prntnode)     {
        lshft = TRUE;
        redist(yp, &trnode);
        write_node(trnode.lfsib, yp);
    }
}
if (lshft == FALSE && trnode.rtsib) {
    read_node(trnode.rtsib, yp);
    if (yp->keyct < bheader[trx].m &&
                yp->prntnode == trnode.prntnode)     {
        rshft = TRUE;
        redist(&trnode, yp);
        write_node(trnode.rtsib, yp);
    }
}
```

continued...

...from previous page

```
free(yp);
if (lshft || rshft) {
    write_node(t, &trnode);
    return OK;
}
p = nextnode();
/* ----------- Split node -------------------- */
if ((bp = (BTREE *) malloc(NODE))==(BTREE *) NULL)  {
    errno = D_OM;
    dberror();
}
set_mem(bp, NODE, '\0');
trnode.keyct = (bheader[trx].m + 1) / 2;
b = (RPTR *)
        (trnode.keyspace+((trnode.keyct+1)*ENTLN)-ADR);
bp->key0 = *b;
bp->keyct = bheader[trx].m - trnode.keyct;
rt_len = bp->keyct * ENTLN;
a = (char *) (b + 1);
mov_mem(a, bp->keyspace, rt_len);
bp->rtsib = trnode.rtsib;
trnode.rtsib = p;
bp->lfsib = t;
bp->nonleaf = trnode.nonleaf;
a -= ENTLN;
mov_mem(a, k, KLEN);
set_mem(a, rt_len + ENTLN, '\0');
if (bheader[trx].rightmost == t)
    bheader[trx].rightmost = p;
if (t == currnode [trx] &&
                currkno [trx]>trnode.keyct) {
    currnode [trx] = p;
    currkno [trx] -= trnode.keyct + 1;
}
ad = p;
sv = t;
t = trnode.prntnode;
if (t)
    bp->prntnode = t;
else    {
```

continued...

...from previous page

```
            p = nextnode();
            trnode.prntnode = p;
            bp->prntnode = p;
        }
        write_node(ad, bp);
        if (bp->rtsib)  {
            if ((yp=(BTREE *)malloc(NODE))==(BTREE *) NULL) {
                errno = D_OM;
                dberror();
            }
            read_node(bp->rtsib, yp);
            yp->lfsib = ad;
            write_node(bp->rtsib, yp);
            free(yp);
        }
        if (bp->nonleaf)
            adopt(&bp->key0, bp->keyct + 1, ad);
        write_node(sv, &trnode);
        if (t)  {
            read_node(t, &trnode);
            a = trnode.keyspace;
            b = &trnode.key0;
            while (*b != bp->lfsib) {
                a += ENTLN;
                b = (RPTR *) (a - ADR);
            }
        }
        free(bp);
    }
    /* -------------------- new root -------------------- */
    if (p == 0)
        p = nextnode();
    if ((bp = (BTREE *) malloc(NODE)) == (BTREE *) NULL)     {
        errno = D_OM;
        dberror();
    }
    set_mem(bp, NODE, '\0');
    bp->nonleaf = nl_flag;
    bp->prntnode = 0;
    bp->rtsib = 0;
```

continued...

...from previous page

```
    bp->lfsib = 0;
    bp->keyct = 1;
    bp->key0 = sv;
    *((RPTR *) (bp->keyspace + KLEN)) = ad;
    mov_mem(k, bp->keyspace, KLEN);
    write_node(p, bp);
    free(bp);
    bheader[trx].rootnode = p;
    if (nl_flag == FALSE)    {
        bheader[trx].rightmost = p;
        bheader[trx].leftmost = p;
        currnode [trx] = p;
        currkno [trx] = 1;
    }
    return OK;
}

/* ----- redistribute keys in sibling nodes ------ */
static void redist(left, right)
BTREE *left, *right;
{
    int n1, n2, len;
    RPTR z;
    char *c, *d, *e;
    BTREE *zp;

    n1 = (left->keyct + right->keyct) / 2;
    if (n1 == left->keyct)
        return;
    n2 = (left->keyct + right->keyct) - n1;
    z = left->prntnode;
    if ((zp = (BTREE *) malloc(NODE)) == FALSE) {
        errno = D_OM;
        dberror();
    }
    c = childptr(right->lfsib, z, zp);
    if (left->keyct < right->keyct) {
        d = left->keyspace + (left->keyct * ENTLN);
        mov_mem(c, d, KLEN);
        d += KLEN;
```

continued...

...from previous page

```
      e = right->keyspace - ADR;
      len = ((right->keyct - n2 - 1) * ENTLN) + ADR;
      mov_mem(e, d, len);
      if (left->nonleaf)
          adopt(d, right->keyct - n2, right->lfsib);
      e += len;
      mov_mem(e, c, KLEN);
      e += KLEN;
      d = right->keyspace - ADR;
      len = (n2 * ENTLN) + ADR;
      mov_mem(e, d, len);
      set_mem(d + len, e - d, '\0');
      if (right->nonleaf == 0 &&
                         left->rtsib == currnode [trx])
          if (currkno [trx] < right->keyct - n2)  {
              currnode [trx] = right->lfsib;
              currkno [trx] += n1 + 1;
          }
          else
              currkno [trx] -= right->keyct - n2;
  }
else    {
      e = right->keyspace+((n2-right->keyct)*ENTLN)-ADR;
      mov_mem(right->keyspace - ADR, e,
                         (right->keyct * ENTLN) + ADR);
      e -= KLEN;
      mov_mem(c, e, KLEN);
      d = left->keyspace + (n1 * ENTLN);
      mov_mem(d, c, KLEN);
      set_mem(d, KLEN, '\0');
      d += KLEN;
      len = ((left->keyct - n1 - 1) * ENTLN) + ADR;
      mov_mem(d, right->keyspace - ADR, len);
      set_mem(d, len, '\0');
      if (right->nonleaf)
          adopt(right->keyspace - ADR,
                         left->keyct - n1, left->rtsib);
      if (left->nonleaf == FALSE)
          if (right->lfsib == currnode [trx] &&
                         currkno [trx] > n1) {
```

continued...

...from previous page

```
                currnode [trx] = left->rtsib;
                currkno [trx] -= n1 + 1;
            }
            else if (left->rtsib == currnode [trx])
                currkno [trx] += left->keyct - n1;
    }
    right->keyct = n2;
    left ->keyct = n1;
    write_node(z, zp);
    free(zp);
}

/* ----------- assign new parents to child nodes ---------- */
static void adopt(ad, kct, newp)
RPTR *ad;
int kct;
RPTR newp;
{
    char *cp;
    BTREE *tmp;

    if ((tmp = (BTREE *) malloc(NODE)) == (BTREE *) NULL)   {
        errno = D_OM;
        dberror();
    }
    while (kct--)   {
        read_node(*ad, tmp);
        tmp->prntnode = newp;
        write_node(*ad, tmp);
        cp = (char *) ad;
        cp += ENTLN;
        ad = (RPTR *) cp;
    }
    free(tmp);
}
```

continued...

...from previous page

```
/* ----- compute node address for a new node -----*/
static RPTR nextnode()
{
    RPTR p;
    BTREE *nb;

    if (bheader[trx].rlsed_node)     {
        if ((nb = (BTREE *) malloc(NODE))==(BTREE *) NULL)  {
            errno = D_OM;
            dberror();
        }
        p = bheader[trx].rlsed_node;
        read_node(p, nb);
        bheader[trx].rlsed_node = nb->prntnode;
        free(nb);
    }
    else
        p = bheader[trx].endnode++;
    return p;
}

/* ----- next sequential key ------- */
RPTR nextkey(tree)
int tree;
{
    trx = tree;
    if (currnode [trx] == 0)
        return firstkey(trx);
    read_node(currnode [trx], &trnode);
    if (currkno [trx] == trnode.keyct)  {
        if (trnode.rtsib == 0)  {
            return (RPTR) 0;
        }
        currnode [trx] = trnode.rtsib;
        currkno [trx] = 0;
        read_node(trnode.rtsib, &trnode);
    }
    else
        currkno [trx]++;
    return *((RPTR *)
```

continued...

...from previous page

```
            (trnode.keyspace+(currkno[trx]*ENTLN)-ADR));
}

/* ----------- previous sequential key ----------- */
RPTR prevkey(tree)
int tree;
{
    trx = tree;
    if (currnode [trx] == 0)
        return lastkey(trx);
    read_node(currnode [trx], &trnode);
    if (currkno [trx] == 0) {
        if (trnode.lfsib == 0)
            return (RPTR) 0;
        currnode [trx] = trnode.lfsib;
        read_node(trnode.lfsib, &trnode);
        currkno [trx] = trnode.keyct;
    }
    else
        currkno [trx]--;
    return *((RPTR *)
        (trnode.keyspace + (currkno [trx] * ENTLN) - ADR));
}

/* ------------- first key ------------- */
RPTR firstkey(tree)
int tree;
{
    trx = tree;
    if (bheader[trx].leftmost == 0)
        return (RPTR) 0;
    read_node(bheader[trx].leftmost, &trnode);
    currnode [trx] = bheader[trx].leftmost;
    currkno [trx] = 1;
    return *((RPTR *) (trnode.keyspace + KLEN));
}
```

continued...

...from previous page

```
/* ------------- last key ---------------- */
RPTR lastkey(tree)
int tree;
{
    trx = tree;
    if (bheader[trx].rightmost == 0)
        return (RPTR) 0;
    read_node(bheader[trx].rightmost, &trnode);
    currnode [trx] = bheader[trx].rightmost;
    currkno [trx] = trnode.keyct;
    return *((RPTR *)
        (trnode.keyspace + (trnode.keyct * ENTLN) - ADR));
}

/* -------- scan to the next sequential key ------ */
static RPTR scannext(p, a)
RPTR *p;
char **a;
{
    RPTR cn;

    if (trnode.nonleaf) {
        *p = *((RPTR *) (*a + KLEN));
        read_node(*p, &trnode);
        while (trnode.nonleaf)  {
            *p = trnode.key0;
            read_node(*p, &trnode);
        }
        *a = trnode.keyspace;
        return *((RPTR *) (*a + KLEN));
    }
    *a += ENTLN;
    while (-1)  {
        if ((trnode.keyspace + (trnode.keyct)
                * ENTLN) != *a)
            return fileaddr(*p, *a);
        if (trnode.prntnode == 0 || trnode.rtsib == 0)
            break;
        cn = *p;
        *p = trnode.prntnode;
```

continued...

...from previous page

```
        read_node(*p, &trnode);
        *a = trnode.keyspace;
        while (*((RPTR *) (*a - ADR)) != cn)
            *a += ENTLN;
    }
    return (RPTR) 0;
}

/* ---- scan to the previous sequential key ---- */
static RPTR scanprev(p, a)
RPTR *p;
char **a;
{
    RPTR cn;

    if (trnode.nonleaf) {
        *p = *((RPTR *) (*a - ADR));
        read_node(*p, &trnode);
        while (trnode.nonleaf)  {
            *p = *((RPTR *)
                (trnode.keyspace+(trnode.keyct)*ENTLN-ADR));
            read_node(*p, &trnode);
        }
        *a = trnode.keyspace + (trnode.keyct - 1) * ENTLN;
        return *((RPTR *) (*a + KLEN));
    }
    while (-1)  {
        if (trnode.keyspace != *a)  {
            *a -= ENTLN;
            return fileaddr(*p, *a);
        }
        if (trnode.prntnode == 0 || trnode.lfsib == 0)
            break;
        cn = *p;
        *p = trnode.prntnode;
        read_node(*p, &trnode);
        *a = trnode.keyspace;
        while (*((RPTR *) (*a - ADR)) != cn)
            *a += ENTLN;
    }
```

continued...

...from previous page

```
    return (RPTR) 0;
}

/* ------ locate pointer to child ---- */
static char *childptr(left, parent, btp)
RPTR left;
RPTR parent;
BTREE *btp;
{
    char *c;

    read_node(parent, btp);
    c = btp->keyspace;
    while (*((RPTR *) (c - ADR)) != left)
        c += ENTLN;
    return c;
}

/* -------------- current key value ---------- */
void keyval(tree, ky)
int tree;
char *ky;
{
    RPTR b, p;
    char *k;
    int i;

    trx = tree;
    b = currnode [trx];
    if (b)  {
        read_node(b, &trnode);
        i = currkno [trx];
        k = trnode.keyspace + ((i - 1) * ENTLN);
        while (i == 0)  {
            p = b;
            b = trnode.prntnode;
            read_node(b, &trnode);
            for (; i <= trnode.keyct; i++)  {
                k = trnode.keyspace + ((i - 1) * ENTLN);
                if (*((RPTR *) (k + KLEN)) == p)
```

continued...

...from previous page

```
                    break;
            }
        }
        mov_mem(k, ky, KLEN);
    }
}

/* -------------- current key ---------- */
RPTR currkey(tree)
int tree;
{
    RPTR f = 0;

    trx = tree;
    if (currnode [trx]) {
        read_node(currnode [trx], &trnode);
        f = *( (RPTR *)
            (trnode.keyspace+(currkno[trx]*ENTLN)-ADR));
    }
    return f;
}

/* ---------- read a btree node ----------- */
static void read_node(nd, bf)
RPTR nd;
BTREE *bf;
{
    bseek(nd);
    read(handle [trx], (char *) bf, NODE);
}

/* ---------- write a btree node ----------- */
static void write_node(nd, bf)
RPTR nd;
BTREE *bf;
{
    bseek(nd);
    write(handle [trx], (char *) bf, NODE);
}
```

continued...

...from previous page

```
/* ----------- seek to the b-tree node ---------- */
static void bseek(nd)
RPTR nd;
{
    if (lseek(handle [trx],
            (long) (NODE+((nd-1)*NODE)),0) == ERROR)      {
        errno = D_IOERR;
        dberror();
    }
}
```

Refer back to the diagram in Figure 6.4. Btree.c is in the symbol that is labeled "B-Tree Index Software."

The B-tree index management functions are valuable utilities that you might find useful in applications other than your data base. The functions in the B-tree library that you can call are described here.

Function build_b:

```
void build_b(name, len)
char *name;
int len;
```

When you want to establish a new B-tree, you will use this function. The **name** parameter points to the name of the B-tree file. The **len** integer is the length of the key value that will be indexed by the B-tree.

Function btree_init:

```
int btree_init(ndx_name)
char *ndx_name;
```

This function initializes processing for an existing B-tree index file. The parameter points to the DOS file name of the B-tree file. The function returns an integer that is used for subsequent calls to the B-tree management functions. That integer is named "tree" in the descriptions of the functions that follow.

Function btree_close:

```
int btree_close(tree)
int tree;
```

This function closes a B-tree that was opened by **btree-init**. This function must be called. The individual B-trees are marked with an "in-use" indicator when they are opened. If your program terminates before **btree-close** is called, this indicator will not be reset, and subsequent attempts to open the B-tree will fail.

Function insertkey:

```
int insertkey(tree, key, ad, unique)
int tree;
char *key;
RPTR ad;
int unique;
```

This function adds a key to the B-tree. The **key** pointer points to the key value to be added. The **ad RPTR** value will be stored with the key and is the value that is returned when the key is located in a search. The **unique** flag tells the function whether or not the B-tree should accept duplicate values. If the flag is non-zero and the value is already in the tree, then the key is not added. If the value is zero, then the key is added, but only if none of the other occurrences of the same key value are stored with an identical **ad RPTR** value.

Function locate:

```
RPTR locate(tree, key)
int tree;
char *key;
```

To find a key value in a B-tree, call **locate**. The tree parameter is the integer that was returned by **btree__init**. The **key** pointer points to the value for which you are searching.

If the key value is in the B-tree, the **RPTR** value that was associated with the key when it was added to the B-tree is returned. If the key value is one of a series of identical values in the B-tree, the **RPTR** is the one that occurs first in the B-tree file.

If the key value is not in the B-tree file, a zero **RPTR** value is returned.

Function deletekey:

```
int deletekey(tree, key, ad)
int tree;
char *key;
RPTR ad;
```

This function is used to delete a key from the B-tree. The **key** pointer points to the value you want to delete. The **ad RPTR** value must match the one that was stored with the key when it was added to the B-tree.

Function firstkey:

```
RPTR firstkey(tree)
int tree;
```

Once a key value has been inserted or when one has been located, the software maintains pointers to the current key location in the B-tree. It is the nature of a B-tree that you can retrieve keys at random or in ascending or descending sequence. The sequential movement through the B-tree can proceed from any key location in the B-tree structure.

The above function returns the **RPTR** value associated with the first key in the collating sequence of the key values of the B-tree. If no keys are stored, the function returns a zero value.

Function lastkey:

```
RPTR lastkey(tree)
int tree;
```

This function returns the **RPTR** value associated with the last key in the collating sequence of the B-tree. If no keys are stored, the function returns a zero value.

Function nextkey:

```
RPTR nextkey(tree)
int tree;
```

If you have already positioned the B-tree pointers by an insertion, deletion, or search, this function retrieves the **RPTR** value associated with the next logical key in the collating sequence of the B-tree. If no B-tree position has been established, this function calls the **firstkey** function.

Function prevkey:

```
RPTR prevkey(tree)
int tree;
```

If you have already positioned the B-tree pointers by an insertion, deletion, or search, this function retrieves the **RPTR** value associated with the previous logical key in the collating sequence of the B-tree. If no B-tree position has been established, this function calls the **lastkey** function.

Function keyval:

```
void keyval(tree, key)
int tree;
char *key;
```

This function retrieves the key value associated with the current key pointer as positioned by the insertion, deletion, or search functions. The retrieved key value is copied into the location pointed to by the **key** pointer. If no key position has been established, no copy is performed.

Function currkey:

```
RPTR currkey(tree)
int tree;
```

This function returns the **RPTR** value associated with the current key pointer as positioned by the insertion, deletion, or search functions. If no key position has been established, a zero **RPTR** value is returned.

Keyboard Header File (keys.h)

Keys.h, shown in Listing 6.16, contains a set of **#define** statements that equate global symbols to the values returned by the IBM PC keyboard when you press the function keys.

(Listing 6.16 on next page)

Listing 6.16 (keys.h)

```
/* ------------------- keys.h ----------------------- */
#define HT 9
#define RUBOUT 8
#define BELL 7
#define ESC 27

#define F1   187
#define F2   188
#define F3   189
#define F4   190
#define F5   191
#define F6   192
#define F7   193
#define F8   194
#define F9   195
#define F10 196

#define HOME    199
#define UP      200
#define PGUP    201
#define BS      203
#define FWD     205
#define END     207
#define DN      208
#define PGDN    209
#define INS     210
#define DEL     211
```

System Subroutines (sys.c)

Listing 6.17 is **sys.c**, a potpourri of system-specific functions that are isolated in this source file to separate the compiler, operating system, and hardware dependencies from the rest of the software. Following are descriptions of sys.c's functions.

Get__char gets a character from the keyboard without the usual keyboard enhancements included when the standard C function **getchar** is used. It also handles the translation of function keys into the integer values as defined in keys.h.

Put__char is the output equivalent of **get__char**. It uses the standard C function named **putchar**, but it allows you to send it the global values **FWD** and **UP** to move the cursor forward one character position or up one line.

Clear__screen clears the screen.

Cursor positions the cursor at a specified character x and y coordinate.

The functions in **sys.c** use the protocols of the ANSI.SYS terminal driver for moving the cursor and clearing the screen. There are faster ways to perform these actions. The IBM PC includes low-level functions in its ROM BIOS that an application program can call for screen and keyboard manipulation. No C language standard exists for using these calls, so the compilers differ in their treatment of the problem. You can use the features of your compiler to access these functions, and you will see an improvement in the performance of these programs' display features. But, in doing so, you will sacrifice a measure of portability. Every indication is that future versions of DOS will require applications programs to obey certain rules in order to function properly in a multi-tasking environment. More than likely, the conventions for Microsoft's Windows environment will resemble those for future versions of DOS. Programs that use the ANSI.SYS protocols work properly in a Windows configuration.

Listing 6.17 (sys.c)

```
/* ---------------- sys.c -------------------- */
#include <stdio.h>
#include "cdata.h"
#include "keys.h"

#if COMPILER == AZTEC
#define ci() scr_getc()
#endif
#if COMPILER == DATALIGHT
#define ci() getch()
#endif
#if COMPILER == ECOC
#define ci() getch()
#endif
#if COMPILER == LATTICE
#define ci() getch()
#endif
#if COMPILER == LETSC
#define ci() getcnb()
#endif
#if COMPILER == MICROSOFT
#define ci() getch()
#endif
#if COMPILER == TURBOC
#define ci() getch()
#endif

/* ------------- get a keyboard character ----------------- */
int get_char()
{
    int c;

#if COMPILER == CI_C86
    c = key_getc();
    if ((c & 255) == 0)
        c = (c >> 8) | 128;
#else
#if COMPILER == WIZARD
    c = bioskey(0);
    if ((c & 255) == 0)
```

continued...

...from previous page

```
        c = (c >> 8) | 128;
#else
    if (!(c = ci()))
        c = ci() | 128;
#endif
#endif
    return c & 255;
}

/* -------- write a character to the screen ------------ */
void put_char(c)
int c;
{
    switch (c)  {
        case FWD:   printf("\033[C");
                    break;
        case UP:    printf("\033[A");
                    break;
        default:    putchar(c);
    }
    fflush(stdout);
}

/* ------------- set the cursor position ------------- */
void cursor(x,y)
int x, y;
{
    printf("\033[%02d;%02dH",y+1, x+1);
    fflush(stdout);
}

/* ------------------- clear the screen ------------------- */
int screen_displayed = 0;
void clear_screen()
{
    screen_displayed = 0;
    printf("\033[2J");
    fflush(stdout);
}
```

SUMMARY

This chapter describes the Cdata Data Base Management System, which is a complete DBMS in that it includes a Data Definition Language and a Data Manipulation Language. To support this DBMS, Chapter 7 presents a package of utility programs. These programs will provide general purpose data base maintenance functions and data management functions that you can call from your programs for record display and reporting.

CHAPTER 7

CDATA UTILITY PROGRAMS

Chapter 6 presented the Cdata data base management system. With it you can design and build a complete software system integrated with a relational data base. To make that task easier, several utility programs are available that provide access to the data base in ways that are common to most data base environments. These programs will reduce the amount of code you must write when you develop an application; they continue in the spirit of software tool building that pervades this work.

In Chapter 6, you learned to include the schema in your application program when you compiled it because the application program talks to the data base, using the globally defined symbols that are a part of the schema. To build the utility programs in this chapter, you compile the data base schema separately. The utility programs are written to use any data base schema; therefore, it is not necessary to recompile them each time you develop a new schema. Rather, you compile the schema as a relocatable object module and link it with the utility programs and the Cdata DML library. This technique applies to all the utility programs.

To compile the Consultant's Billing System schema from Chapter 6, build the source file shown in Listing 7.1. Compile it separately, and then compile the particular utility program you want to build. Link them both with the Cdata DML library. This procedure builds an executable version of the utility program customized for the specific data base schema.

Listing 7.1 (cbs.c)

```
/* ------------- cbs.c ---------------- */

#include "cbs.c1"
#include "cbs.c2"
#include "cbs.c3"
```

THE DATA BASE SIZE CALCULATOR (DBSIZE.C)

After designing a data base, you need to know how much disk storage it requires. You might be thinking about storing it on a diskette or a small capacity hard disk. You could be sharing space with other software and data. Whatever the reason, you need a method for estimating the storage requirements. Knowing the data and index file formats and guessing at the data file volumes, you could sit down with a calculator and figure it out yourself. But there is a better way. Since the storage required for a Cdata data base is a function of the number of records in each file and the number of indexes into each file, a program is included that calculates the disk space from estimates of the file sizes. The program is named **dbsize.c** and is shown in Listing 7.2.

(Listing 7.2 on next page)

Listing 7.2 (dbsize.c)

```
/* -------------------- dbsize.c ------------------------ */
/*  Compute the character size of a database */

#include <stdio.h>
#include "cdata.h"

void index_m();

main()
{
    int f, x;
    long rct [MXFILS];              /* number of records/file  */
    long fsize [MXFILS];            /* file sizes              */
    long dsize = 0;                 /* data base sizes         */
    int m [MXINDEX];                /* btree m values          */
    long xsize [MXFILS] [MXINDEX];  /* index sizes             */

    for (f = 0; dbfiles [f]; f++)    {
        printf("\nEnter record count for %-10s: ",dbfiles[f]);
        fflush(stdout);
        scanf("%ld", &rct [f]);
        fsize [f] = rct [f] * rlen(f) + sizeof(FHEADER);
        printf("File size:                     %10ld",
                         fsize [f]);
        dsize += fsize [f];
        index_m(f, m);
        for (x = 0; m [x]; x++) {
            xsize [f] [x] = (2 + (rct [f] / m [x])) * NODE;
            dsize += xsize [f] [x];
            printf(
                "\nIndex %d (m=%2d) size:               %10ld",
                    x+1,m[x],xsize[f][x]);
        }
    }
    printf("\n                                    ----------");
    printf("\nData base size:                %10ld", dsize);
}
```

continued...

...from previous page

```
/* --- compute the btree m values
            for the indices of a data base file --- */
static void index_m(f, m)
int f;              /* file number */
int *m;             /* array of m values */
{
    int x, x1;
    int len;

    for (x = 0; x < MXINDEX; x++)    {
        *m = 0;
        if (index_ele [f] [x] [0] == 0)
            break;
        len = 0;
        for (x1 = 0; index_ele [f] [x] [x1]; x1++)
            len += ellen [index_ele [f] [x] [x1] - 1];
        *m++ = ((NODE-(sizeof(int)*2)
                -sizeof(RPTR)*4))/(len+sizeof(RPTR));
    }
}
```

To run the program, type its name: dbsize. The program will then ask you about the number of records in each file. Dbsize uses your answers to calculate the data file and index file storage requirements. Screen 7.1 shows this program being run against the CBS schema.

```
C>dbsize

Enter record count for CLIENTS    : 12
File size:                                      1366
Index 1 (m=54) size:                            1024
Enter record count for PROJECTS   : 25
File size:                                      1210
Index 1 (m=54) size:                            1024
Enter record count for CONSULTANTS: 10
File size:                                       330
Index 1 (m=54) size:                            1024
Enter record count for ASSIGNMENTS: 35
File size:                                       640
Index 1 (m=35) size:                            1536
Index 2 (m=54) size:                            1024
Index 3 (m=54) size:                            1024
                                          ----------
Data base size:                                10202
```

Screen 7.1   Dbsize Session for CBS Schema

DATA BASE INITIALIZATION (DBINIT.C)

After you have designed a data base schema and before your applications programs can access the data base, you must build initial copies of the data and index files with no records in them. The program **dbinit.c** performs this task for you. When run, it initializes the entire data base. If a copy of the data base already exists, dbinit erases it and replaces the copy with the new, empty data base. The program is shown in Listing 7.3.

Listing 7.3 (dbinit.c)

```
/* --------------- dbinit.c ------------------------ */

/* This program is used to build the initial data base.
   It constructs all files and indexes.
   There is no data loaded,
   and any existing files are deleted.    */

#include <stdio.h>
#include "cdata.h"

extern char *dbfiles [];
extern void file_create();

main ()
{
    int f = 0;
    extern int rlen();
    char fname [13];

    while (dbfiles [f]) {
        sprintf(fname, "%.8s.dat", dbfiles [f]);
        file_create(fname, rlen(f));
        printf("\nCreating file %s with length %d",
                              fname, rlen(f));
        build_index("", f);
        f++;
    }
}
```

To run dbinit, type its name. Screen 7.2 shows a dbinit session that uses the CBS data base schema to initialize the CBS data base.

```
C>dbinit

Creating file CLIENTS.dat with length 120
Creating file PROJECTS.dat with length 48
Creating file CONSULTA.dat with length 32
Creating file ASSIGNME.dat with length 18
```

Screen 7.2 Dbinit Session for CBS Data Base

DATA ENTRY AND QUERY (QD.C)

Except for the invoice program that served as an example in Chapter 6, no software has been developed to access the data in the data base files. Later, you will write some custom programs, but, for now, you just want to store, look at, change, and delete some records in files.

When you develop an on-line application, you code data entry and retrieval programs. Many of these programs are logically similar but differ in the files accessed and the data elements involved. The user enters the primary key data element value for the record desired, and the program displays the record. The user moves the cursor around the screen and changes data element values. Then the user tells the program to store that record and get another one. Maybe the user deletes a record or adds a new one. The process is universal; most DBMS packages include a program that allows the user to browse the data base, doing all the things just mentioned.

Cdata has such a program. It is called **qd.c** and is shown in Listing 7.4. **Qd** allows you to specify a file and, optionally, a list of data elements. It constructs a data entry screen, displays it, and waits for you to key in the primary key data element. You can use a list of data elements on the command line when you execute **qd**, but you must include the primary key data element as the first one. Screen 7.3 shows a session using **qd** with the CLIENTS file in the CBS data base. It shows (a) the command line that tells **qd** to display the client number, phone number, and amount due from the file of clients. Then it shows (b) the screen template built by **qd**. In the next screen (c), the user has entered the client number 00015. The last screen (d) shows the record that **qd** has retrieved.

```
a.  C>qd clients client_no client_name phone amt_due


b.                      --- CLIENTS ---
    CLIENT NO           _____
    CLIENT NAME         _____
    PHONE               (___)___-____
    AMT DUE             $_____.__


c.                      --- CLIENTS ---
    CLIENT NO           00015
    CLIENT NAME         _____
    PHONE               (___)___-____
    AMT DUE             $_____.__


d.                      --- CLIENTS ---
    CLIENT NO           00015
    CLIENT NAME         Ace_Wrecking_Yard_____
    PHONE               (305)123-4567
    AMT DUE             $__1500.00
```

Screen 7.3 A qd Session with the CLIENTS File

Once **qd** has retrieved a record, you can change its data by moving the cursor among the data element fields and changing the data values. When you are satisfied with the record's new contents, press the function key F1 to return the changed record to the data base. The **qd** program displays an empty template, and you can start again. To reject any changes you have made to a record, press the [Esc] key rather than F1.

You can display the previous or the next record on the screen by using function keys PgUp and PgDn. Pressing the PgUp key at the beginning of the file causes **qd** to display the first record in the key sequence. Pressing the PgDn key at the end of the file displays the last record. If you use the PgUp or PgDn keys after you have changed data values in the current record, **qd** writes the new record to the data base in place of the original and then retrieves the previous or next record. Use the Home and End keys to display the first and last record in the file.

You can use **qd** to add and delete records from the data base. If you enter a primary key that does not exist, **qd** displays the message, "Adding new record." If you did not mean to add a new record — perhaps you entered the wrong primary key value — then press the [Esc] key to reject the addition. If you did mean to add a record, you can enter data values into the data element fields. Press the F1 key when the data values are correct.

To delete a record using **qd**, enter its key value and review the record that **qd** retrieves. Then press the F7 key (the delete function key). **Qd** displays a message that says, "Verify w/F7." This message tells you to verify your delete request by pressing the F7 key a second time. **Qd** deletes the record and displays an empty template. If you press something other than the F7 key, qd rejects the delete request.

The cursor arrow keys, the Enter key, and the Tab key move the cursor around the screen. Use the Ins key to toggle the Insert mode. In the Insert mode, you can insert characters into a field. Each keystroke shifts the characters on the right of the cursor one position to the right. When Insert mode is off, the new keystrokes overwrite the characters under the cursor. Use the Del key to delete the character under the cursor. Use the Backspace key to delete the character to the left of the cursor.

To exit **qd**, press the [Esc] key when the template is empty.

Table 7.1 is a summary of the keyboard functions for qd. Listing 7.4 for the **qd.c** program follows.

```
F1              Write a changed/new record
                  to the data base.
F7              Delete a record from the data base.
PgUp            View the previous record.
PgDn            View the next record.
Home            View the first record.
End             View the last record.
Esc             (When record is visible)
                  Reject any additions/changes.
                  Clear the template.
                (When template is empty)
                  Exit from qd.
Ins             Toggle keyboard Insert mode
Tab             Move cursor to next field
Enter             "      "    "    "      "
Down Arrow        "      "    "    "      "
Up Arrow        Move cursor to previous field
Right Arrow     Move cursor right one character
Left Arrow      Move cursor left one character
Backspace <-    Delete character to left of cursor
Del             Delete character under cursor
```

Table 7.1 Summary of qd Keyboard Functions

(Listing 7.4 on next page)

Listing 7.4: (qd.c)

```
/* ------------------------ qd.c --------------------- */
/* A query program.  Enter the name of the data base file and
 * (optionally) a list of data elements.  A screen is built
 * and the file is updated based upon the data entered.
 */
#include <stdio.h>
#include "keys.h"
#include "cdata.h"

static int file;
int existing_record;
char *rb;                /* record buffer */
char *hb;                /* hold buffer */
char *sc;                /* screen buffer   */
int len;                 /* record length   */
char *malloc();
int fl[] = {0, -1};
int iplist [MXELE+1];
int *els;
void query(), rcdin(), rcdout(), set_trap(), clear_record();
int key_entry();

main(argc, argv)
int argc;
char *argv[];
{
    if (argc > 1)   {
        if ((file = filename(argv[1])) != ERROR)     {
            if (argc == 2) {
                len = rlen(file);
                els = file_ele [file];
            }
            else if (ellist(argc-2, argv+2, iplist) == OK)  {
                len = epos(0, iplist);
                els = iplist;
            }
            else
                exit(1);
            sc = malloc(len);          /* screen buffer */
            rb = malloc(rlen(file));    /* record buffer */
```

continued...

...from previous page

```
            hb = malloc(rlen(file));    /* hold buffer   */
            if (sc == (char *) 0 ||
                    rb == (char *) 0 ||
                        hb == (char *) 0)    {
                printf("\nOut of memory");
                exit(1);
            }
            init_rcd(file, rb);
            init_rcd(file, hb);
            init_screen(argv[1], els, sc);
            query();
            free(hb);
            free(rb);
            free(sc);
        }
    }
}




/* -------------- process the query ------------ */
static void query()
{
    int term = 0;

    *fl = file;
    db_open("", fl);
    clrrcd(sc, els);
    set_trap();
    while (term != ESC) {
        term = data_entry();
        switch (term)    {
            /* ----------- GO --------------- */
            case F1:    rcdout();
                        break;
            /* ------------- First record ---------- */
            case HOME:  rcdout();
                        if (first_rcd(file, 1, rb) == ERROR)
                            post_notice("Empty file");
                        else
```

continued...

...from previous page

```
                rcdin();
            break;
/* ------------- First record ---------- */
case END:   rcdout();
            if (last_rcd(file, 1, rb) == ERROR)
                post_notice("Empty file");
            else
                rcdin();
            break;
/* ------------- Previous record -------- */
case PGUP:  rcdout();
            if (prev_rcd(file, 1, rb) == ERROR) {
                post_notice("Beginning of file");
                if (first_rcd(file, 1, rb) ==
                                        ERROR)  {
                    post_notice("Empty file");
                    break;
                }
            }
            rcdin();
            break;
/* ------------- Next record ------------- */
case PGDN:  rcdout();
            if (next_rcd(file, 1, rb) == ERROR) {
                post_notice("At end of file");
                if (last_rcd(file, 1, rb) ==
                                        ERROR)  {
                    post_notice("Empty file");
                    break;
                }
            }
            rcdin();
            break;
/* ------------- Delete record ------------- */
case F7:    if (spaces(rb)== 0) {
                post_notice("Verify w/F7");
                if (get_char() == F7)    {
                    del_rcd(file);
                    clear_record();
                }
```

continued...

...from previous page

```
                              clear_notice();
                    }
                    break;
          case ESC:   if (spaces(sc))
                          break;
                      clear_record();
                      term = 0;
                      break;
          default:    break;
        }
    }
    clear_screen();
    db_cls();
}

/* ----------- clear out the record area -------------- */
static void clear_record()
{
    int i = 0;
    while (index_ele [file] [0] [i])
        protect(index_ele[file][0][i++],FALSE);
    clrrcd(sc, els);
    existing_record = FALSE;
}

/* ----------- get the data base file record ------------ */
static void rcdin()
{
    int i = 0;

    if (empty(rb, rlen(file)) == 0) {
        rcd_fill(rb, sc, file_ele [file], els);
        mov_mem(rb, hb, rlen(file));
        existing_record = TRUE;
        while (index_ele [file] [0] [i])
            protect(index_ele[file][0][i++],TRUE);
    }
}
```

continued...

...from previous page

```
/* ------- add or update the data base file record ------ */
static void rcdout()
{
    if (empty(sc, len) == 0)     {
        rcd_fill(sc, rb, els, file_ele[file]);
        if (existing_record)     {
            if (same() == 0)     {
                post_notice("Returning record");
                rtn_rcd(file, rb);
            }
        }
        else     {
            post_notice("New record added");
            if (add_rcd(file, rb) == ERROR)
                dberror();
        }
        clear_record();
    }
}

/* -------- test for an empty record buffer ---------- */
static int empty(b, l)
char *b;
int l;
{
    while (l--)
        if (*b && *b != ' ')
            return FALSE;
        else
            b++;
    return TRUE;
}

/* ---------- test two record buffers for equality ------- */
static int same()
{
    int ln = rlen(file);

    while (--ln)
        if (*(rb + ln) != *(hb + ln))
```

continued...

...from previous page

```
            break;
    return (*(rb + ln) == *(hb + ln));
}

/* ------ set the query screen's key element trap --------- */
static void set_trap()
{
    int i = 0;

    while (index_ele [file] [0] [i])
        i++;
    edit(index_ele [file] [0] [i-1], key_entry);
}

/* --- come here when the primary key has been entered ---- */
static int key_entry(s)
char *s;
{
    char key [MXKEYLEN];
    int i;

    if (spaces(s))
        return OK;
    *key = '\0';
    i = 0;
    while (index_ele [file] [0] [i])    {
        protect(index_ele[file][0][i],TRUE);
        strcat(key, sc + epos(index_ele[file][0][i++], els));
    }
    if (find_rcd(file, 1, key, rb) == ERROR)    {
        post_notice("New record");
        existing_record = FALSE;
        return OK;
    }
    rcdin();
    tally();
    return OK;
}
```

DATA BASE FILE REPORT PROGRAM (DS.C)

Most automated systems include printed reports taken from the data in the data base files. As you develop applications software, you address the requirements for specific reports. But before you can satisfy those requirements, you need a report program that lists the contents of the data files. As with the **qd** program, the report program should be general enough to allow you to specify a file and the data elements that you want to show on the report.

To meet this reporting requirement, a program called **ds.c** is provided as shown in Listing 7.5. You run it using the same command line format as in the **qd** program. You may redirect the output to the printer or display it on the screen. Use the PC-DOS I/O redirection convention to send the report to the printer. (Type " >prn" on the command line along with the parameters. See your *PC-DOS User's Guide* for details on I/O redirection.) The program senses which output you've chosen and acts accordingly; it causes a page eject for the printer or pauses and waits for a keystroke when the screen is full. The program also restricts a screen display to an 80-column format, truncating at the data element level. Reports directed to the printer may be up to 136 characters long. Screen 7.4 (following Listing 7.5) shows the command line and resulting report when **ds** reports the PROJECTS file from the CBS data base. Even though all the data elements from the file are shown, their arrangement on the report line is different from their arrangement in the file, which shows how you can use the command line to select specific data elements for the report.

Listing 7.5 (ds.c)

```c
/* ----------------------- ds.c ----------------------- */

/*  Display the data of a file on stdout.  Type the filename
 *  and a list of data element names.  The query response is
 *  sent to the standard output device.  If no element list
 *  is typed, the query uses the format of the file record.
 */

#include <stdio.h>
#include "cdata.h"

main(argc, argv)
int argc;
char *argv[];
{
    int f, iplist [MXELE+1];
    static int fl [] = {0, -1};
    extern void dblist();

    if (argc > 1)    {
        if ((f = filename(argv[1])) != ERROR)    {
            *fl = f;
            db_open("", fl);
            if (argc == 2)
                dblist(stdout, TRUE, f, 1, file_ele [f]);
            else if (ellist(argc - 2, argv + 2, iplist) == OK)
                dblist(stdout, TRUE, f, 0, iplist);
            db_cls();
        }
    }
}
```

```
C>ds projects client_no project_no project_name amt_expended

Filename: PROJECTS
CLIENT_NO PROJECT_NO PROJECT_NAME              AMT_EXPENDED
--------- ---------- ------------------------- ------------
00022     00001      Payroll                   $  12250.00
00022     00002      Inventory                 $  10295.00
00022     00003      General Ledger            $   7501.00
Records: 3

C>
```

Screen 7.4 General Report Program (ds)

If you do not specify data elements on the command line, the **ds** program uses all the data elements in the file's schema and reports the records in the sequence of the primary key. If you specify selected data elements, the report is in the physical order of the records in the file and displays only the data elements you specify.

If the report line does not fit on a display line (80 columns on the screen, 132 columns on the printer), **ds** truncates the rightmost data elements.

Ds calls the function named **dblist** to prepare the display or report output. Because **dblist** is a useful tool for applications programs, it is described and listed separately.

INDEX BUILDER (INDEX.C)

You use this utility program when you have had a problem, which occurs most often during testing. After the system is operational, you use the index program mainly to recover from power failures, but when you are testing and blowing up programs, you use it often.

The inverted index files of Cdata use B-tree algorithms. If a program terminates without bringing the indexes to an orderly close, the system locks the B-trees. This measure is correct because the trees are unreliable if they have not been properly closed. The next time you try to use them, Cdata will sense this condition.

The only correct measure is to rebuild the indexes by running the program named **index.c** shown in Listing 7.6. Make sure that **index.exe** is available on the default DOS subdirectory whenever one of your Cdata applications programs is running.

You can run this program anytime you are in doubt about the integrity of an index. You can run it against a particular file in the data base or against all of the files. To run index, enter its name followed either by the word "all" or by a list of data base file names as shown here:

```
C>index all
C>index projects clients
```

(Listing 7.6 on next page)

Listing 7.6 (index.c)

```
/* -------------------- index.c ---------------------- */
#include <stdio.h>
#include "cdata.h"
extern RPTR curr_a [];  /* current record file address  */

main (argc, argv)
char *argv [];
{
    int f = 1, i;
    static int fs [MXFILS+1];
    char *malloc(), *bf, *path;

    if (argc < 2)    {
        printf("\nFile name or 'all' required");
        exit();
    }
    if (strcmp("all", argv [1]) == 0)   /* index all */
        for (f = 0; dbfiles [f]; f++) /* put files in list */
            fs [f] = f;
    else if ((*fs = filename(argv[1])) == ERROR)
        exit();
    fs [f] = (-1); /* terminator (file,file,...,-1) */
    path = argc > 2 ? argv[2] : "";
    /* delete and rebuild indexes
                in the data base files being indexed */
    for (i = 0; (f = fs [i]) != (-1); i++)
        build_index(path, f);
    /* Open the data base files. */
    db_open(path, fs);
    for (i = 0; (f = fs [i]) != (-1); i++)  {
        printf("\nIndexing %s", dbfiles [f]);
        bf = malloc(rlen(f));
        while (seqrcd(f, bf) != ERROR)
            add_indexes(f, bf, curr_a [f]);
        free(bf);
    }
    db_cls();
}
```

The **index** program calls the function named **filename** to parse the file names that you enter on the command line. You will find this function discussed in Chapter 6.

SOME USEFUL UTILITY FUNCTIONS

The utility programs in this chapter use several functions that are described here. They are separated from the programs because you can use them in the development of applications programs. This aspect qualifies them as tools in the toolset and, as such, they are maintained apart from the programs that use them.

Parse Command Line Data Element List (ellist.c)

Function ellist:

```
int ellist(count, names, list)
int count;          /* number of names in the list */
char *names[];      /* the names */
int *list;          /* the resulting list */
```

Remember in Chapter 6 that Cdata describes a record by using an array of data element global integers terminated with an integer of zero value. Remember also that the names of the data elements are defined in an array of pointers to ASCII strings. The function named **ellist** (Listing 7.7) converts a list of ASCII data element names into an integer array similar to a Cdata record definition array. This function allows you to specify queries and reports with a selected set of data elements on the command line. The utility programs **qd** and **ds** both use this function.

Call **ellist**, passing it the number of names in the list and the address of an array of character pointers that point to the names. Also, pass it the address of an integer array where the resulting record-defining array will be built.

Ellist will return **OK** if the list is properly built and **ERROR** if one of the names in the strings is not a valid data element name. If **ellist** finds an error, it displays an error message on the console before it returns.

Listing 7.7 (ellist.c)

```
/* ---------------------- ellist.c ---------------------- */

/*
 *   Construct list of data element tokens from list of names
 *   such as might be entered on a command line.
 *   Return OK, or ERROR if one of the names is not in the
 *   dictionary.
 */

#include <stdio.h>
#include "cdata.h"

int ellist(count, names, list)
int count;                    /* number of names in the list */
char *names[];                /* the names */
int *list;                    /* the resulting list */
{
    char elname [31];
    int el, el1;
    extern void name_cvt();

    for (el = 0; el < count; el++)  {
        for (el1 = 0; ; el1++)  {
            if (denames [el1] == (char *) 0)     {
                fprintf(stderr,
                    "\nNo such data element as %s", elname);
                return ERROR;
            }
            name_cvt(elname, names[el]);
            if (strcmp(elname, denames [el1]) == 0)
                break;
        }
        *list++ = el1 + 1;
    }
    *list = 0;
    return OK;
}
```

Screen Manager (screen.c)

The screen manager functions (Listing 7.8) are, in the jargon of the popular software media, "powerful and sophisticated," which conjures up the image of an incredible hulk in a tuxedo. The screen functions are the mainstay of the **qd** program, and they do quite a bit of work. They use the record definition conventions of Cdata to manage data entry into a screen template.

The screen functions build temporary screen templates for ad hoc data entry and query programs. The data elements are displayed one per line. See the programs **posttime.c** and **payments.c** in Chapter 8 for examples of how applications programs can use the screen functions.

Each function uses a caller-supplied list of data elements and a data entry collection buffer.

Following is a description of the functions in the Screen Management toolset that applications programs can call.

Function init_screen:

```
init_screen(name, elist, bf)
char *name;     /* template name */
int *elist;     /* data element list */
char *bf;       /* data entry buffer */
```

The **init__screen** function initializes the screen processing software for a particular entry screen format. The **name** string pointer points to a string that **init__screen** will display at the top of the screen. **Elist** points to a null-terminated array of data element integers. The screen manager uses the array to select the names and entry masks for the template from the data base schema. **Bf** points to a data buffer into which the screen manager will collect the data values. The buffer must be long enough to hold all the data elements in the list. Data entry processes will write data elements into the buffer in the sequence of the list.

Function protect:

```
protect(el, tf)
int el;        /* field data element */
int tf;        /* true to protect */
```

The screen manager treats data element fields on the template as "protected" or "unprotected." You can enter data into an unprotected field but not into a protected field. To protect or unprotect a field, you call this function before any data entry occurs and after you have called **init__screen**. Use the data element global name as the first parameter and either a true value or a false value to tell the function to protect or unprotect the field.

Function edit:

```
edit(el, func)
int el;           /* field data element */
int (*func)();    /* edit function to call */
```

You can tell the screen manager to call a custom function when the data entry is complete for a specific data element, which will allow you to validate the entry or to use a key element to retrieve a record from the data base. Use the data element global integer name as the first parameter and a pointer to your custom function as the second. Your function must return the integer value OK if the data value is correct or ERROR if it is not. The header file **cdata.h** defines these values.

Function display_template:

```
display_template()
```

Call this function to display the template on the screen. Since the **data__entry** function described next calls **display__template** automatically, you will need this call only if you have changed the screen display.

Function data_entry:

```
int data_entry()
```

Call this function to allow the user to enter data into the screen template and, therefore, into the buffer you identified when you called **init__screen**. The function will call **display__crt** and **tally** (described next) to display the template and any data element values in the buffer before data entry begins.

Function tally:

```
tally()
```

This function displays data values that are in the buffer on the template. You can use this call in your custom edit function. First, retrieve the record that matches a key data element value. Next, move the record's data element values into the screen buffer. Then call **tally**.

Function put_field:

```
put_field(el)
int el;          /* field data element */
```

Call **put__field** to display the current value of a specified data element on the screen template. You will use this function to display any data element that you have computed or changed from within your program.

Listing 7.8 (screen.c)

```c
/* ---------------- screen.c ------------------------ */
#include <stdio.h>
#include "cdata.h"
#include "keys.h"

int insert_mode = FALSE;        /* insert mode, TRUE/FALSE */
extern int prev_col, prev_row;  /* current cursor location */
extern int screen_displayed;    /* template displayed flag */
#define FIELDCHAR '_'           /* field filler character  */

struct {
    int prot;
    int (*edits)();
} sb [MXELE];

int *elist;
char *bf;
char *tname;
void right_justify(),
    right_justify_zero_fill(), left_justify_zero_fill(),
    disp_element(), insert_status(),
    put_fchar(), data_coord();

/* ----------- initialize the screen process ------------- */
void init_screen(name, els, bfr)
char *name;
int *els;
char *bfr;
{
    tname = name;
    elist = els;
    bf = bfr;
}

/* ------- set the protect flag for a screen field ------- */
void protect(el, tf)
int el, tf;
{
    sb[elp(el)].prot = tf;
}
    continued...
```

...from previous page

```
/* ---- set the field edit function for a screen field --- */
void edit(el, func)
int el, (*func)();
{
    sb[elp(el)].edits = func;
}

/* ---- compute the relative position
            of an element on a screen ------ */
static int elp(el)
int el;
{
    int i;

    for (i = 0; *(elist + i); i++)
        if (el == *(elist + i))
            break;
    return i;
}

/* ----------- Display the crt template ----------- */
void display_template()
{
    int i, el, ct;
    char detag[16], *cp1, *cp2;

    clear_screen();
    screen_displayed = TRUE;
    ct = no_flds();
    printf("\n                    --- %s ---\n", tname);
    for (i = 0; i < ct; i++)     {
        el = *(elist + i) - 1;
        cp1 = denames[el];
        cp2 = detag;
        while (*cp1 && cp2 < detag + sizeof detag - 1)  {
            *cp2++ = *cp1 == '_' ? ' ' : *cp1;
            cp1++;
        }
        *cp2 = '\0';
```

continued...

...from previous page

```
        printf("\n%-16.16s %s",detag, elmask[el]);
    }
    printf("\n");
    insert_status();
}

/* ----- Process data entry for a screen template. ---- */
int data_entry()
{
    int (*validfunct)();
    int field_ctr, exitcode, el;
    int field_ptr = 0, done = FALSE, isvalid;
    char *bfptr;

    if (screen_displayed == 0)
        display_template();
    tally();
    field_ctr = no_flds();
    /* ---- collect data from keyboard into screen ---- */
    while (done == FALSE)    {
        bfptr = bf + epos(elist[field_ptr], elist);;
        el = *(elist + field_ptr) - 1;
        validfunct = sb[field_ptr].edits;
        data_coord(el + 1);
        if (sb[field_ptr].prot == FALSE)     {
            exitcode =
                read_element(eltype[el], elmask[el], bfptr);
            isvalid = (exitcode != ESC && validfunct) ?
                        (*validfunct)(bfptr,exitcode) : OK;
        }
        else    {
            exitcode = FWD;
            isvalid = OK;
        }
        if (isvalid == OK)
            switch (exitcode)    {         /* passed edit */
                case DN:                   /* cursor down key */
                case '\r':                 /* enter/return */
                case '\t':                 /* horizontal tab */
                case FWD:                  /* -> */
```

continued...

...from previous page

```
                    if (field_ptr+1 == field_ctr)
                        field_ptr = 0;
                    else
                        field_ptr++;
                    break;
                case UP:                    /* cursor up key */
                case BS:                    /* back space */
                    if (field_ptr == 0)
                        field_ptr = field_ctr - 1;
                    else
                        field_ptr--;
                    break;
                default:
                    done = endstroke(exitcode);
                    break;
            }
    }
    return (exitcode);
}

/* ----- Compute the number of fields on a template ------ */
static int no_flds()
{
    int ct = 0;

    while (*(elist + ct))
        ct++;
    return ct;
}

/* ------ compute data element field coordinates --------- */
static void data_coord(el)
int el;
{
    prev_col = 17;
    prev_row = elp(el) + 3;
}
```

continued...

...from previous page

```
/* ------- read data element from keyboard ------------- */
static int read_element(type, msk, bfr)
char type, *msk, *bfr;
{
    char *mask = msk, *buff = bfr;
    int done = FALSE, c, column = prev_col;

    while (*mask != FIELDCHAR)  {
        prev_col++;
        mask++;
    }
    while (TRUE)    {
        cursor(prev_col, prev_row);
        c = get_char();
        clear_notice();
        switch (c)  {
            case '\b':
            case BS:
                if (buff == bfr)    {
                    done = c == BS;
                    break;
                }
                --buff;
                do  {
                    --mask;
                    --prev_col;
                } while (*mask != FIELDCHAR);
                if (c == BS)
                    break;
            case DEL:
                mov_mem(buff+1, buff, strlen(buff));
                *(buff+strlen(buff)) = ' ';
                cursor(prev_col, prev_row);
                disp_element(buff,mask);
                break;
            case FWD:
                do  {
                    prev_col++;
                    mask++;
                } while (*mask && *mask != FIELDCHAR);
```

continued...

...from previous page

```
            buff++;
            break;
        case INS:
            insert_mode ^= TRUE;
            insert_status();
            break;
        case '.':
            if (type == 'C')    {
                if (*mask++ && *buff == ' ')    {
                    *buff++ = '0';
                    if (*mask++ && *buff == ' ')
                        *buff++ = '0';
                }
                right_justify(bfr);
                cursor(column, prev_row);
                disp_element(bfr, msk);
                prev_col = column + strlen(msk)-2;
                mask = msk + strlen(msk)-2;
                buff = bfr + strlen(bfr)-2;
                break;
            }
        default:
            if (endstroke(c))   {
                done = TRUE;
                break;
            }
            if (type != 'A' && !isdigit(c)) {
                error_message("Numbers only");
                break;
            }
            if (insert_mode)    {
                mov_mem(buff, buff+1, strlen(buff)-1);
                disp_element(buff,mask);
            }
            *buff++ = c;
            put_fchar(c);
            do  {
                prev_col++;
                mask++;
            } while (*mask && *mask != FIELDCHAR);
```

continued...

...from previous page

```
                if (!*mask)
                    c = FWD;
                break;
        }
        if (!*mask)
            done = TRUE;
        if (done)    {
            if (type == 'D' &&
                c != ESC &&
                    validate_date(bfr) != OK)
                return -1;
            break;
        }
    }
    if (c != ESC && type != 'A')     {
        if (type == 'C')    {
            if (*mask++ && *buff == ' ')     {
                *buff++ = '0';
                if (*mask++ && *buff == ' ')
                    *buff++ = '0';
            }
        }
        if (type == 'Z' || type == 'D')
            right_justify_zero_fill(bfr);
        else
            right_justify(bfr);
        cursor(column, prev_row);
        disp_element(bfr,msk);
    }
    return (c);
}

/* ---------- test c for an ending keystroke ----------- */
endstroke(c)
{
    switch (c) {
        case '\r':
        case '\n':
        case '\t':
        case ESC:
```

continued...

...from previous page

```
        case F1:
        case F2:
        case F3:
        case F4:
        case F5:
        case F6:
        case F7:
        case F8:
        case F9:
        case F10:
        case PGUP:
        case PGDN:
        case HOME:
        case END:
        case UP:
        case DN:
            return TRUE;
        default:
            return FALSE;
    }
}

/* ------- right justify, space fill -------- */
static void right_justify(s)
char *s;
{
    int len;

    len = strlen(s);
    while (*s == ' ' || *s == '0' && len)   {
        len--;
        *s++ = ' ';
    }
    if (len)
        while (*(s+(len-1)) == ' ') {
            mov_mem(s, s+1, len-1);
            *s = ' ';
        }
}
```

continued...

...from previous page

```
/* ---------- right justify, zero fill --------------- */
static void right_justify_zero_fill(s)
char *s;
{
    int len;

    if (spaces(s))
        return;
    len = strlen(s);
    while (*(s + len - 1) == ' ')    {
        mov_mem(s, s + 1, len-1);
        *s = '0';
    }
}

/* ----------- test for spaces -------- */
int spaces(c)
char *c;
{
    while (*c == ' ')
        c++;
    return !*c;
}

/* -------------- validate a date ----------------- */
static int validate_date(s)
char *s;
{
    static int days [] =
        { 31,28,31,30,31,30,31,31,30,31,30,31 };
    char date [7];
    int mo;

    strcpy(date, s);
    if (spaces(date))
        return OK;
    if (!atoi(date + 4))
        days[1]++;
    *(date + 4) = '\0';
    mo = atoi(date+2);
```

continued...

...from previous page

```
    *(date+2) = '\0';
    if (mo && mo < 13 && atoi(date) &&
                atoi(date) <= days [mo - 1])
        return OK;
    error_message("Invalid date");
    return ERROR;
}

/* ---- display all the fields on a screen ------ */
void tally()
{
    int *els = elist;

    while (*els)
        put_field(*els++);
}

/* ------- write a data element on the screen --------- */
void put_field(el)
int el;
{
    data_coord(el);
    cursor(prev_col, prev_row);
    disp_element(bf + epos(el, elist), elmask[el - 1]);
}

/* ---------- display a data element -------- */
static void disp_element(b, msk)
char *b, *msk;
{
    while (*msk)    {
        put_fchar(*msk != FIELDCHAR ? *msk : *b++);
        msk++;
    }
    cursor(prev_col,prev_row);
}
```

continued...

229

...from previous page

```
/* ---------- display insert mode status ------------------ */
static void insert_status()
{
    cursor(65,24);
    printf(insert_mode ? "[INS]" : "       ");
    cursor(prev_col,prev_row);
}


/* --------- write a field character --------- */
static void put_fchar(c)
int c;
{
    put_char(c == ' ' ? '_' : c);
}
```

File-Listing Utilities

Function dblist:

```
dblist(f, k, list)
int f;        /* file number */
int k;        /* key number  */
int *list;    /* list of elements */
```

The **ds** program calls **dblist** (Listing 7.9) to prepare a listing or screen display of the contents of the file named on the command line. The **dblist** program manages the production of the output. You can call the same function from within an applications program. When you do, pass it the global file integer, a key number, and the list of data element integers that you want selected from the file. The key number determines the sequence of the output. If the key number is zero, the output will be in the physical sequence of the records in the file; otherwise, the key number specifies the primary key (1) or one of the secondary keys (2, 3, and so on), and the output will be in the sequence of the chosen key index.

Listing 7.9 (dblist.c)

```c
/* -------------------- dblist.c ----------------------- */
#include <stdio.h>
#include "cdata.h"
extern char *malloc();
extern int free();

void dblist(fd, inter, f, k, list)
FILE *fd;    /* output file */
int inter;   /* true for user interaction and page breaks */
int f;       /* file number */
int k;       /* key number */
int *list;   /* list of elements */
{
    char *bf;
    int rcdct = 0;
    extern void clist(), test_eop(), oflow();
    bf = malloc(rlen(f));
    errno = 0;
    if (k)
        first_rcd(f, k, bf);
    if (inter == 0)
        oflow(fd, FALSE, dbfiles [f], list);
    while (errno != D_EOF) {
        if (k)  {
            clist(fd,inter,file_ele[f],list,bf,dbfiles[f]);
            rcdct++;
            next_rcd(f, k, bf);
        }
        else if (seqrcd(f, bf) != ERROR)    {
            clist(fd,inter,file_ele[f],list,bf,dbfiles[f]);
            rcdct++;
        }
    }
    if (inter)  {
        test_eop(fd, dbfiles [f], list);
        fprintf(fd, "\nRecords: %d\n", rcdct);
    }
    free(bf);
}
```

Function clist:

```
clist(fl, pl, bf, fn)
int *fl;      /* file list */
int *pl;      /* print list */
char *bf;     /* buffer     */
char *fn;     /* file name  */
```

The **dblist** function calls the **clist** function (Listing 7.10) to list or display individual records. It can be useful in applications programs as well. **Dblist** produces a display of a record as described by the data element file list parameter. Data elements are taken from the memory location pointed to by the buffer parameter and are assumed to be in the format specified by the file list. The function produces an appropriate header line of data element names along with a title taken from the file name parameter. It knows whether output is going to the printer or the screen, and it issues a page eject at the end of a printed page or pauses at the bottom of a screen.

You can use this function to display the result of any kind of data selection as long as all the data elements in the record are in the Cdata data element dictionary.

Listing 7.10 (clist.c)

```c
/* --------------------- clist.c -------------------- */

#include <stdio.h>
#include "cdata.h"

#define SCRNLINES 20
#define PRNTLINES 55

int lct = 99;
int clip;

/* ------------ list a record ----------- */

/* Send 2 lists; a list of elements in buffer and a list of
 * elements to be listed. Also send address of the buffer.
 * Can be used to list a data base file or an extract file.
 */

void clist(fd, inter, fl, pl, bf, fn)
FILE *fd;          /* output file */
int inter;         /* true for user interaction & page breaks */
int *fl;           /* file list  */
int *pl;           /* print list */
char *bf;          /* buffer     */
char *fn;          /* file name  */
{
    char *ln, *cp, *mp, *malloc();
    int width;
    int lw = 0;
    void test_eop();

    ln = malloc(epos(0, pl) + 1);
    clip = ((!inter || isatty(fileno(fd))) ? 79 : 136);
    if (inter)
        test_eop(fd, fn, pl);
    rcd_fill(bf, ln, fl, pl);
    cp = ln;
    if (*pl)    {
        putc('\n', fd);
        putc('\r', fd);
```

continued...

...from previous page

```
        lct++;
    }
    while (*pl) {
        mp = elmask [(*pl) - 1];
        width = hdlen(*pl++);
        lw += width + 1;
        if (lw >= clip)
            break;
        while (width--)    {
            if (*mp && *mp != '_')
                putc(*mp, fd);
            else if (*cp)   {
                putc(isprint(*cp) ? *cp : '?', fd);
                cp++;
            }
            else
                putc(' ', fd);
            if (*mp)
                mp++;
        }
        if (*pl)
            putc(' ', fd);
        cp++;
    }
    free(ln);
}

/* ----------- test for end of page/screen --------- */
void test_eop(fd, fn, pl)
FILE *fd;
char *fn;        /* file name */
int *pl;         /* element list */
{
    void oflow();

    if (lct >= (isatty(fileno(fd)) ? SCRNLINES : PRNTLINES))
        oflow(fd, TRUE, fn, pl);
}
```

continued...

...from previous page

```
/* -------------- top of page/screen ------------ */
void oflow(fd, inter, fn, pl)
FILE *fd;
char *fn;        /* file name */
int *pl;         /* element list */
{
    int width;
    int *ll;
    int ow = 0;
    char msk [80];

    clip = ((!inter || isatty(fileno(fd))) ? 79 : 136);
    ll = pl;
    if (inter && lct < 99)  {
        if (isatty(fileno(fd))) {
            printf("\n<cr> to continue...");
            while (get_char() != '\r')
                ;
        }
        else
            printf("\r\f");
    }
    lct = 0;
    if (inter && isatty(fileno(fd)))
        clear_screen();
    if (inter)
        fprintf(fd, "Filename: %s\n", fn);
    while (*pl) {
        width = hdlen(*pl);
        ow += width + 1;
        if (ow >= clip)
            break;
        sprintf(msk, "%%-%d.%ds ", width, width);
        fprintf(fd, msk, denames [(*pl++) - 1]);
    }
    ow = 0;
    putc('\n', fd);
    putc('\r', fd);
    while (*ll) {
        width = hdlen(*ll++);
```

continued...

...from previous page

```
        ow += width + 1;
        if (ow >= clip)
            break;
        while (width--)
            putc('-', fd);
        putc(' ', fd);
    }
}

static int hdlen(el)
int el;
{
    el--;
    return strlen(elmask [el]) < strlen(denames [el]) ?
        strlen(denames [el]) :
        strlen(elmask [el]);
}

/* ---------- isatty function
            for the compilers that do not have it ------ */
#if COMPILER == ECOC
isatty(fd)
{
    int dev;

    dev = ioctl(fd, 0, 0);
    if ((dev & 0x80) == 0)
        return FALSE;
    return (dev & 3);
}
#endif

#if COMPILER == CI_C86
#include <dos.h>
struct regval rg;

isatty(fd)
{
    rg.ax = 0x4400;
    rg.bx = fd;
```

continued...

...from previous page

```
    sysint(0x21, &rg, &rg);
    if ((rg.dx & 0x80) == 0)
        return FALSE;
    return (rg.dx & 3);
}
#endif

#if COMPILER == DATALIGHT
#include <dos.h>
REGS rg;

int isatty(fd)
int fd;
{
    rg.ax = 0x4400;
    rg.bx = fd;
    int86(0x21, &rg, &rg);
    if ((rg.dx & 0x80) == 0)
        return FALSE;
    return (rg.dx & 3);
}
#endif

#if COMPILER == LETSC
#include <dos.h>
struct reg rg;

int isatty(fd)
int fd;
{
    rg.r_ax = 0x4400;
    rg.r_bx = fd;
    intcall(&rg, &rg, 0x21);
    if ((rg.r_dx & 0x80) == 0)
        return FALSE;
    return (rg.r_dx & 3);
}
#endif
```

continued...

...from previous page

```
#if COMPILER == WIZARD
int isatty(fd)
int fd;
{
    int dev;

    dev = ioctl(fd, 0, 0, 0);
    if ((dev & 0x80) == 0)
        return FALSE;
    return (dev & 3);
}
#endif
```

Parse File Name

Function filename:

```
int filename(fn)
char *fn;    /* file name to convert */
```

Just as you must convert data element names to their integer equivalents, so must you convert file names. The **qd**, **ds**, and **index** utility programs all use the file name as you enter it on the command line when you execute the program. They then call the function named **filename** to get the file integer that the Cdata DML functions recognize. **Filename** returns the integer if the file name is a valid one and the value **ERROR** if it is not. If you pass an incorrect file name, **filename** will display an error message on the console before it returns.

Filename is found in Listing 6.13 in Chapter 6.

Function name_cvt:

```
int name_cvt(c1, c2)
char *c1, *c2;
```

The function **name__cvt** is also in Listing 6.13. It converts a string to uppercase letters. The first parameter is the address of the string for the converted data. The second parameter is the address of the string to be converted. This function is mentioned here because several utility programs use it, and even though the function is small, it is useful.

SUMMARY

You have now finished building the Cdata data base management system, complete with data definition language, data manipulation language, and utility functions. The software described in these chapters is real; it is used in many installations. Large, complex applications systems have been built with no more tools than these programs, an editor, and a compiler. To illustrate the flexibility and usability of this approach, Chapter 8 presents a small application, the Consultant's Billing System. This simple but functional application uses the data base design presented in this book for examples of the Cdata approach.

CHAPTER 8

AN APPLICATION: THE CONSULTANT'S BILLING SYSTEM

This chapter presents the primary objective of this book: to develop a software system to support an application. This exercise involves using the data base designed in earlier chapters—a data base that supports a billing system for a consulting firm.

Begin by considering the requirements for such a system. In actual practice, the requirements analysis is the first step in the design of a computer system. In this chapter, it is postponed until the discussion of the software that surrounds the data base.

CONSULTANT'S BILLING SYSTEM REQUIREMENTS

A Consultant's Billing System must maintain records of consultants, clients, and projects. Since consultants work on and charge time to the projects of clients, the system will relate consultants to projects and projects to clients. A consultant might charge different rates for different projects, so the system records a rate for each consultant-to-project assignment. The system also provides for hourly charges and other direct expenses against a project, posts payments when they occur, and even prepares invoices.

CONSULTANT'S BILLING SYSTEM SOFTWARE DESIGN

Figure 8.1 shows the structure chart of a likely Consultant's Billing System. This system seems simple. The data base design in the previous chapters is sufficient to support the requirements of the Consultant's Billing System; all it needs are some programs to process the data. With the Cdata DBMS, you already have most of the programs written. The Consultant's Billing System uses the utility programs from Chapter 7, the Cdata functions from Chapter 6, and three custom applications programs. There are only three new programs, and one of them was written in Chapter 6—the **invoice** program used to illustrate how you build applications programs around Cdata. To understand how a complete application can be built with only three custom programs, consider the individual processes a user of a Consultant's Billing System will require.

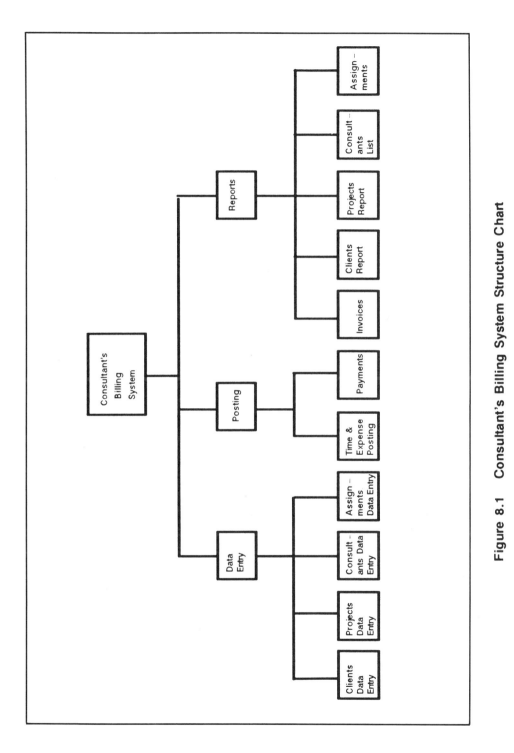

Figure 8.1   Consultant's Billing System Structure Chart

Consultant's Billing System Data Entry

To enter data into the Consultant's Billing System, you need a data base. At first, the data base is empty; it has no records. Before you can begin, you must build the empty data base. The **dbinit** utility program initializes a data base that you describe in the Cdata format. That program builds an empty data base. Then, you need a way to enter data into each of the files. You must add clients, consultants, and projects to the data base, and you must also assign consultants to projects. Occasionally, you will want to change the data values of existing records or delete records from the data base. You want to do what the **qd** utility program does; therefore, most of your data entry requirements are supported by this existing program, the **qd** utility.

The data entry process for the CLIENTS file can illustrate this technique. Each CLIENTS file consists of the client number, name, address, phone number, and the amount of money the client owes the consulting firm. Normal data entry will be done for all the data elements except the amount due, which is always a function of time and expenses expended against the client's projects and payments received from the client. File maintenance for the client records will include all the data elements in the file except the amount due.

To use the **qd** program for data entry into the CLIENTS file, you can build a DOS batch file that contains the following set of commands:

```
qd clients client_no client_name address city state zip phone
```

This file is named CLNTENTR.BAT. To run data entry for the clients file, enter the command **clntentr** on the DOS command line and observe the display shown in Screen 8.1.

```
                        --- clients ---

        CLIENT NO       _____
        CLIENT NAME     _____
        ADDRESS         _____
        CITY            _____
        STATE           __
        ZIP             _____
        PHONE           (___)___-____
```

Screen 8.1 CLIENTS File Data Entry Screen

Using the same approach, you can build the following batch files to execute data entry for the PROJECTS file, the CONSULTANTS file, and the ASSIGNMENTS file:

```
Batch File        Command
_____       _____

PROJENTR.BAT      qd projects
CONSENTR.BAT      qd consultants
ASGNENTR.BAT      qd assignments
```

Each of these processes allows data entry on all the data elements in the file that **qd** reads.   Screens 8.2 through 8.4 are the data entry screens generated by these commands:

```
                        --- projects ---

        PROJECT NO      _____
        PROJECT NAME    _____
        AMT EXPENDED    $_____.__
        CLIENT NO       _____
```

Screen 8.2 PROJECTS File Data Entry Screen

```
                        --- consultants ---

    CONSULTANT NO     _____
    CONSULTANT NAME   _____
```

Screen 8.3 CONSULTANTS File Data Entry Screen

```
                        --- assignments ---

    CONSULTANT NO     _____
    PROJECT NO        _____
    RATE           $____.__
```

Screen 8.4 ASSIGNMENTS File Data Entry Screen

Consultant's Billing System Reports

Just as the **qd** utility program manages routine data entry into the Consultant's Billing System, the **ds** utility program supports most of the reporting requirements. The Consultant's Billing System contains five basic reports. The first four are reports for the contents of the four files and the last is a report for the preparation of invoices. The discussion of the invoice program will be deferred until later; for now, concentrate on the listings of the file contents. Each of these listings is produced by the **ds** utility program. By using the batch files shown here, you can produce the reports shown in Listings 8.1 through 8.4:

```
Batch File   Command
_____

CLNTREPT.BAT ds clients client_no client_name phone amt_due >prn
PROJREPT.BAT ds projects >prn
CONSREPT.BAT ds consultants >prn
ASGNREPT.BAT ds assignments >prn
```

Listing 8.1

```
Filename: CLIENTS
CLIENT_NO CLIENT_NAME                        PHONE           AMT_DUE
--------- ------------------------------     -------------   ----------
00001     Smith Engineering                  (703)555-6453 $   1980.00
00002     Jones Dairy                        (703)555-2345 $    500.00
00003     Harry's Auto Mart                  (703)555-9876 $       .
Records: 3
```

Listing 8.2

```
Filename: PROJECTS
PROJECT_NO PROJECT_NAME                   AMT_EXPENDED CLIENT_NO
---------- -------------------------      ------------ ---------
00001      Payroll Analysis              $   2500.00   00001
00002      General Ledger                $   1480.00   00001
00003      Inventory System              $   1000.00   00002
00004      Hardware Market Survey        $       .     00002
Records: 4
```

Listing 8.3

```
Filename: CONSULTANTS
CONSULTANT_NO CONSULTANT_NAME
------------- -------------------------
00001         George Martin
00002         Sam Spade
00003         Phil Napolean
00004         Barney Fife
Records: 4
```

Listing 8.4

```
Filename: ASSIGNMENTS
CONSULTANT_NO PROJECT_NO RATE
------------- ---------- -------
00001         00001      $ 40.00
00001         00002      $ 40.00
00001         00004      $ 40.00
00002         00001      $ 35.00
00002         00004      $ 35.00
00003         00002      $ 37.00
00003         00003      $ 37.00
00004         00003      $ 25.00
Records: 8
```

Notice that you direct the reports to the printer by using the input/output redirection facility of PC-DOS. You can display these same reports on the screen by eliminating the expression "＞prn" from each of the commands.

The Data Posting Programs

Three kinds of data values are posted to the Consultant's Billing System data base. Data entry (discussed earlier) and data posting are differentiated in this manner; data entry involves the nonroutine maintenance of data in the data base, and data **posting** implies routine transactions that support the purpose of the system. When you change a client's phone number, that is data entry. When you add a consultant to the file, that is data entry. Data entry appends data values to the data base or replaces data values that already exist. Data posting adjusts existing data values in the data base, often with addition or subtraction. The three data values to be posted to the data base are listed here:

- Labor hours charged to projects
- Expenses charged to projects
- Payments received from clients

These processes are beyond the abilities of the Cdata utility programs and require algorithms not implied by the schema, so you need custom programs to support them. A program named **posttime.c** (Listing 8.5) manages the posting of hours and expenses. This program is an example of using multiple files in a data base. When you enter a consultant number, the program reads the CONSULTANTS file to find the consultant's name. Then, when you enter a project number, the program retrieves the project name from the PROJECTS file. The program displays each of these names just after retrieving it. If you have entered a valid consultant and a valid project, the program reads the ASSIGNMENTS file to determine if the consultant is assigned to the project. If not, an error message appears; otherwise, the program retrieves the hourly rate for the selected consultant on the selected project. After you have entered hours and expenses, the program uses the client number in the projects file to find the associated CLIENTS record. The amount to charge is computed as hours × rate + expenses. This amount is added to the amount due in the client record and the amount expended in the project record.

(Listing 8.5 on next page)

Listing 8.5 (posttime.c)

```c
/* ------------------ posttime.c -------------------- */
#include <stdio.h>
#include "keys.h"
#include "cdata.h"
#include "cbs.c1"

char *sc;
char *malloc();
int fl[] = {CLIENTS, CONSULTANTS, PROJECTS, ASSIGNMENTS, -1};
int els [] = {CONSULTANT_NO, CONSULTANT_NAME,
              PROJECT_NO, PROJECT_NAME, HOURS, EXPENSE, 0};
struct clients cl;
struct consultants cs;
struct projects pr;
struct assignments as;

main()
{
    int term = '\0';
    int edcons(), edproj();
    long atol();
    long exp, rt, time_chg;
    int hrs;

    db_open("", fl);
    sc = malloc(epos(0, els));
    clrrcd(sc, els);
    init_screen("Time & Expenses", els, sc);
    edit(CONSULTANT_NO, edcons);      /* consultant number   */
    protect(CONSULTANT_NAME, TRUE);   /* consultant name     */
    edit(PROJECT_NO, edproj);         /* project number      */
    protect(PROJECT_NAME, TRUE);      /* project name        */
    while (term != ESC) {
        term = data_entry();
        switch (term)   {
            /* ----------- GO --------------- */
            case F1:
                hrs = atoi(sc + epos(HOURS, els));
                exp = atol(sc + epos(EXPENSE, els));
```

continued...

...from previous page

```
                rt = atol(as.rate);
                time_chg = rt * hrs;
                clrrcd(sc, els);
                sprintf(cl.amt_due, "%8ld",
                        atol(cl.amt_due)+time_chg+exp);
                rtn_rcd(CLIENTS, &cl);
                sprintf(pr.amt_expended, "%9ld",
                        atol(pr.amt_expended)+time_chg+exp);
                rtn_rcd(PROJECTS, &pr);
                break;
            case ESC:
                if (spaces(sc))
                    break;
                clrrcd(sc, els);
                term = '\0';
                break;
            default:
                break;
        }
    }
    clear_screen();
    free(sc);
    db_cls();
}

/* -------- consultant number ---------- */
edcons(s)
char *s;
{
    if (find_rcd(CONSULTANTS, 1, s, &cs) == ERROR)  {
        dberror();
        return ERROR;
    }
    rcd_fill(&cs, sc, file_ele[CONSULTANTS], els);
    put_field(CONSULTANT_NAME);
    return OK;
}
```

continued...

...from previous page

```
/* -------- project number ---------- */
edproj(s)
char *s;
{
    char consproj [11];

    if (find_rcd(PROJECTS, 1, s, &pr) == ERROR) {
        dberror();
        return ERROR;
    }
    rcd_fill(&pr, sc, file_ele[PROJECTS], els);
    put_field(PROJECT_NAME);
    strcpy(consproj, cs.consultant_no);
    strcat(consproj, pr.project_no);
    if (find_rcd(ASSIGNMENTS, 1, consproj, &as) == ERROR)   {
        error_message("Consultant not assigned to project");
        return ERROR;
    }
    find_rcd(CLIENTS, 1, pr.client_no, &cl);
    return OK;
}
```

The program named **payments.c** (Listing 8.6) posts client payments and accesses the CLIENTS file. It retrieves the client record by using the client number that you enter. The payment amount is compared to the amount due. If the payment is greater than the amount due, an over-payment error message appears; otherwise, the program subtracts the payment amount from the amount due in the client record.

Listing 8.6 (payments.c)

```
/* ------------------ payments.c -------------------- */

#include <stdio.h>
#include "keys.h"
#include "cdata.h"
#include "cbs.c1"

char *sc;
char *malloc();
int fl[] = {CLIENTS, -1};
int els [] =
    {CLIENT_NO, CLIENT_NAME, AMT_DUE, PAYMENT, DATE_PAID, 0};
struct clients cl;
int len;

main()
{
    int term = '\0';
    int edcl();
    long atol();

    db_open("", fl);
    len = epos(0, els);
    sc = malloc(len);
    clrrcd(sc, els);
    init_screen("Payments", els, sc);
    edit(CLIENT_NO, edcl);
    protect(CLIENT_NAME, TRUE);
    protect(AMT_DUE, TRUE);
    while (term != ESC) {
        term = data_entry();
        switch (term)   {
            case F1:
                if (atol(cl.amt_due) <
                        atol(sc + epos(PAYMENT, els)))  {
                    error_message("Overpayment");
                    continue;
                }
                sprintf(cl.amt_due,"%8ld",
                    atol(cl.amt_due)
```

continued...

253

...from previous page

```
                    -atol(sc+epos(PAYMENT,els)));
                clrrcd(sc, els);
                rtn_rcd(CLIENTS, &cl);
                break;
            case ESC:
                if (spaces(sc))
                    break;
                clrrcd(sc, els);
                term = '\0';
                break;
            default:
                break;
        }
    }
    clear_screen();
    free(sc);
    db_cls();
}


/* -------- client number ---------- */
edcl(s)
char *s;
{
    if (find_rcd(CLIENTS, 1, s, &cl) == ERROR)  {
        dberror();
        return ERROR;
    }
    rcd_fill(&cl, sc, file_ele[CLIENTS], els);
    tally();
    return OK;
}
```

The Invoice Program

This last program completes the Consultant's Billing System and generates invoices for clients. The **invoice** program was used in Chapter 6 as an example of applications programs that use a Cdata data base, so you will find a listing of its source code in Chapter 6. When you type its name on the command line, the program prepares statements showing the current amount due from each client. Listing 8.7 is an example of the statements produced by the **invoice** program.

Listing 8.7

```
Invoice for Services Rendered

Smith Engineering
1212 Mecca Ave
Vienna                      , VA 22101

Amount Due: $    1980.00



Invoice for Services Rendered

Jones Dairy

Bristow                     , VA 22111

Amount Due: $     500.00



Invoice for Services Rendered

Harry's Auto Mart
123 King St
Alexandria                  , VA 22333

Amount Due: $       0.00
```

SUMMARY

The Consultant's Billing System is not a complete accounting system. It lacks the accounting detail and control mechanisms that a medium-sized or large consulting firm requires for adequate record maintenance. It works for a small consulting firm that limits its practice to a few clients and projects. It does, however, provide a compact example of the use of the Cdata approach to data base management. Do not let this small example lead you to think that Cdata is only applicable to small or simple applications. Cdata is routinely used in much larger and more complex systems.

CHAPTER 9

BUILDING THE SOFTWARE

This chapter discusses how to build the programs that are published in this book by using one of the several C compilers for the PC.

C COMPILERS

The following table lists the compilers with which the code published in this book can be compiled. These compilers, and those that were tested and not used, are individually discussed later in this chapter.

Compiler	Version	Vendor	Location	Phone
Aztec C86	3.40B	Manx Software Systems	Shrewsbury, NJ	(800) 221-0440
C-86	2.30J	Computer Innovations	Tinton Falls, NJ	(201) 542-5920
Datalight C	2.03	Datalight	Seattle, WA	(800) 221-6630
Eco-C88	3.13	Ecosoft	Indianapolis, IN	(800) 952-0472
Lattice C	3.20	Lattice	Glen Ellyn, IL	(312) 858-7950
Let's C	3.0.2	Mark Williams Co.	Chicago, IL	(800) 692-1700
Microsoft C	4.0	Microsoft	Bellevue, WA	(800) 426-9400
Turbo C	Beta	Borland	Scotts Valley, CA	(800) 255-8008
Wizard C	3.0	Wizard Systems	Monte Sereno, CA	(408) 224-6015

List prices for these compilers range from $60 to $500, and a product can have several prices depending on its optional packages; however, the list price is not often paid. Several software mail order dealers offer substantial discounts. These dealers advertise in most of the magazines that are aimed at programmers.

The Differences Between Compilers

Although the differences between compilers are minor, the source code must, necessarily, be able to adjust itself for those small differences. If you always work with the same compiler, you can remove the code that manages these differences.

A global identifier named COMPILER is used in the source code to identify the compiler being used. At compile time, this identifier is set on the command line that executes the compiler. All the compilers allow you to simulate a coded **#define** statement on the command line. Later in this chapter, batch files that build the software with each of the compilers are covered. These files include a control statement to set the COMPILER identifer.

The **compiler identifer** is used in **#if** preprocessor statements in several source files to alter the compilation to match the compiler being used. These statements can be found in **cdata.h**, **schema.c**, **datafile.c**, **btree.c**, **clist.c**, and **sys.c**.

In cdata.h, the COMPILER identifier controls the inclusion of two header files. Most compilers have header files named **errno.h** and **fcntl.h**, and the Cdata software uses them; however, Let's C, Lattice C, and CI-C86 do not have **errno.h**; Let's C, Datalight C, and CI-C86 do not have **fcntl.h**, so the COMPILER directive causes the **#include** statements for these compilers to be ignored.

The C language and its function library are being defined in an ANSI standard, and the compiler vendors all claim compliance. But one area where no agreement has been reached is in the parameters for the **open**, **fopen**, and **creat** functions. (Only the **fopen** function is part of the coming ANSI standard — a mistake, but a reality, nonetheless.) These functions include parameters that specify the access privileges and the text or binary mode of the file being created or opened. In text mode, the newline character is expanded into a carriage return-line feed sequence for output, and the carriage return-line feed sequence is collapsed into a newline character when the record is read. In binary mode, no translation occurs in either direction.

It seems that every compiler has implemented a different set of values for the text and binary parameters. As a result, the COMPILER directive is used in **cdata.h** to provide values for the Cdata global identifiers — CMODE and OPENMODE. These values are then substituted in the Cdata functions that call the affected library functions. To get global identifiers for the correct values, you must include the header files **types.h** and **stat.h** for Microsoft C and **stat.h** for Turbo C. No other compiler requires these files, so the COMPILER identifer is used to include the required files for these two compilers.

A further complication is caused by the Lattice compiler. It cannot create a file in the binary mode with the open function and leave it open for reading and writing unless the global integer named __iomode is set to the values 0x8000. The Lattice compiler's documentation says it can perform this function, but it hasn't worked for several versions of the compiler. This circumstance is why functions in **btree.c** and **datafile.c** set the __iomode integer, use the creat function to create a file, then close it, and then open it. For these programs, this sequence is the only one that works with the Lattice compiler.

Computer Innovations C-86 does not have the **void** function type, so **cdata.h** redefines this value to **int** for that compiler only. C-86 also has a strange convention. Rather than include the usual **atol** function that converts an ASCII string to its equivalent long-integer value, C-86 uses its **atoi** (ascii-to-integer) function for that purpose. It seems that **atoi** is really **atol**, and if the calling function is expecting an integer, it only gets half of the result, ignoring the most significant 16 bits. This strategy is clever, but silly; therefore, cdata.h uses the COMPILER identifer to tell it to substitute the function name **atoi** for any **atol** calls.

Four of the nine compilers include a useful function named **isatty** that returns a true value if a file handle is assigned to the console and a false value if it is not. The Cdata utilities use this function to see if a report is being sent to the screen, to the printer, or to a file. Since the screen is limited to 80 characters, the truncation of the output line is adjusted for this limit rather than the 132-character width of the printer. Because Eco-C88, CI-C86, Datalight, Let's C, and Wizard C do not include the **isatty** function, it is included in the source file clist.c where it is used. Since the **isatty** function needs to make direct BIOS calls, and since each compiler makes these calls differently, the **isatty** function is different for each compiler.

The Wizard C compiler uses an unconventional **strncmp** function. It does not work like every other **strncmp** function in the C world; therefore, a correct **strncmp** function is included in the program schema.c where it is used. This function is compiled only for the Wizard compiler.

The **screen.c** program that Cdata uses for queries requires an unadorned console input function. This function must read the keyboard without echoing the keyed value to the screen and without scanning for special control sequences such as Ctrl-Z or Ctrl-X. It must also return a single, distinguishable value for each of the function keys. Most compilers provide a function that can be used this way, but several do not, and those that do provide one have no standard way of doing so; therefore, the COMPILER identifer is used in the **sys.c** source file to establish this capability for each of the compilers.

Choosing a Compiler

The software in this book can be compiled and run by using the C compilers that are listed at the beginning of this chapter. Later, you will learn how to build the software by using each of these compilers.

Although the software was originally developed for use in a specific compiler environment, it was soon ported to others. As use of the software spread to other installations, other compilers were involved. Eventually, the code was tested with most PC C compilers. With a few exceptions, all the compilers proved able to support this code.

Time overtakes events, and computer products improve. The reasons for not using some of the compilers may have changed by the time you read this book. These reasons are mainly related to the techniques that are used in the Cdata approach to data base descriptions or to small incompatibilities between compilers.

Where compilers differ, the largest common denominator was chosen to support the most compilers. Those compilers known to be in widest use were given preference so that this work could be used immediately by more programmers.

If a preference is shown for a particular compiler, it is because the author is comfortable with it as a result of long experience. All the compliers are suitable for developing software in the C language in the PC environment. Some have features not seen in others, and there are cost considerations; however, you should be willing to accept a programming assignment that involves the use of any of them. This judgement has qualifications. Not all compilers support large memory models (more about this topic later), so your choice of a compiler should be made in view of the size of the problem you are trying to solve.

If you read what seem to be deficiencies in a particular compiler — ones that would influence your decision to use it — you should verify that those deficiencies still exist. This chapter is not meant to be a product review such as you will read in a programmer's magazine. Magazines have a practical life expectancy of one month, and their opinions and reactions to products are expected to be old news even by the time the issue is published. A book should outlast the versions of software it discusses.

If features or deficiencies in some compilers are overlooked, it is because of the author's limited experience with that product. Most of this software was mature and reliable before it was compiled by these compilers, and the debugging tools or quirks of some of the compilers are not addressed here.

The following discussions will identify those characteristics of each particular compiler that necessitated code changes to accommodate it, or that eliminated it from use in this project. You should be able to modify this code to work with most of the compilers that were eliminated, and the modifications should be minor. They are not published here because to do so would clutter the listings with too many compiler-dependent conditionals, thus obscuring the meaning of the code and the purpose for this book; however, the discussion of a particular compiler will tell you what you must do to use it. Once again, you are reminded that these conclusions could be old news by the time you read this book. Compare your version of a compiler to the one that was used in this project, and see if the newer release changes some of these results.

The sections that follow explain some of the features that compilers may or may not have. When these features are mentioned in reference to particular compiler discussions that conclude this chapter, you will then understand those features more concretely.

Assemblers

An **assembler** program translates assembly language source code into machine language suitable for input to the linker. (Linkers are discussed next.) Most compilers have an assembler pass, but not all of them provide the assembler program in a form you can use to assemble your own assembly language code. Those compilers that do not provide such a program often use an internal format of tokens rather than the usual mnemonic assembly language.

One compiler, QC88, does not include an assembler program, even though it compiles to standard Microsoft or IBM assembly language. Using QC88 requires that you purchase your assembler program from another source. QC88 is a hacker's compiler, one that includes the source code for the compiler itself. As such, it is targeted for the kind of audience who can be expected to have an assembler program already.

Some compilers do not reveal to you the assembly language they compile. This lack of information will prevent you from internally optimizing the compiled code. It also prevents you from verifying that a compiler is compiling incorrect code when you suspect it.

Linkers

When you compile a C program, the compilation process builds a relocatable object module. This module contains the machine language code for the source module being compiled. This module cannot be executed by itself. It lacks the startup functions that most C compilers use, and it has none of the code for any library functions that the program calls. Since an executable program can be built from several independently compiled C source programs, and since the startup and library code is not compiled every time you compile a source file, a process is needed that combines all the separate object modules together into one executable module. This process is called a **linker**.

DOS includes a linker program along with its operating system utilities. This program, named LINK.EXE, is a generic linker, able to link the output from any language compiler or assembler that generates relocatable object modules in the proper format. With LINK.EXE, you can link object files that are compiled from many different languages.

Some of the C compilers rely on LINK.EXE to link their programs, and their function libraries and compiled object modules conform to the DOS format. Other compilers provide their own linker programs and use unique formats that do not conform to the DOS standard. Some of these compilers have options that allow you to convert their files to the DOS format. Others provide compile options that generate a DOS object file.

A unique linker can have its advantages. The Aztec linker can tell if you are mixing memory models. Most compiler-unique linkers know the location and name of the startup code, so you don't need to specify that information on the link command line. Some also know the location and names of the standard function libraries.

A unique linker with no DOS-complying compilation or conversion option will prevent you from linking with programs other than those built with the vendor's compiler or assembler. This limitation could be a disadvantage. On the other hand, these linkers tend to be faster than LINK.EXE.

Debuggers

A **debugger** is a program that assists you in debugging another program. The DOS utility, DEBUG.COM, is an example of a debugger. DEBUG.COM is an assembly language debugger at the lowest level. You can debug a program by stepping through the machine instructions, setting breakpoints, and looking at and changing memory and registers.

More advanced debuggers provide symbolic debugging, which means that you can specify functions and variables by their source code names rather than by their compiled memory locations. For these programs to work, the compilers must insert symbolic information into the object modules — information about variable and function names that does not interfere with the execution of the program. The compilers also insert source code line numbers, which the debuggers use to relate the current code execution circumstances to the source files.

The latest generation of debuggers works with the actual source files as well. They display the source code lines on the screen during execution and program stepping. For these debuggers to work, the source files must be available and must not have been changed since the program was compiled and linked. The more advanced of these debuggers provide a full-screen display of the source file as the program is executed.

Some compilers include debuggers as standard equipment. Others provide them as extra cost options. Some compilers have no debugger of their own but include options to compile and link the controls that are supported by other debuggers available from third-party vendors.

The oldest C debugger is the **printf** function. Judicious placement of **printf** statements can track down the most elusive logic errors. There are newer, faster ways to debug, but, rather than take the time to learn the syntax of a new debugger, many programmers still use **printf** to test a program being developed for a new compiler.

The subject of debugging is a book in itself. The next generation of compilers will emphasize the use of full-screen, source-level debuggers in an interactive software development environment. The debuggers will be integrated with the compilers and editors, all using fancy displays of pop-down windows, context-sensitive error messages, and fast compile and link times. No one will consider using a compiler that is not integrated in this way.

The problem with today's debuggers is that they use a good deal of memory and can mask the problem you are trying to debug; nonetheless, debuggers, at any level, are indispensable. This author has used two of them—the **printf** function and Microsoft's Codeview debugger. Codeview is so easy and natural to use that a problem piece of C code will get ported to Microsoft C so Codeview can be used to debug it.

One compiler, Datalight, has recently used advertising space in the national press to challenge Microsoft to a benchmark duel, measuring compile and execution speeds. A better measure, and one Microsoft would currently win would be a measure of the elapsed time required to develop a complex software system. Datalight has no debugger, and Microsoft has Codeview. Everything else being the same, the difference in programmer labor hours would be significant.

Memory Models

The 8088/8086/80286 microprocessor family has what is called a **segmented memory architecture**. Programs can address memory using a 16-bit address, and 16 bits is enough of an address to support only 64K (65536) bytes of memory. To get beyond this limit, the microprocessor adds four **segment registers** that are used to extend the address to a 20-bit width, thus giving a range of 1 megabyte of memory. The extended address is computed by shifting the 16-bit segment register four bits to the left and adding in the 16-bit address offset. Usually, the segment registers have constant values, and the offsets are encoded in the program. There are separate segment registers for code (CS), data (DS), and the stack (SS), and one extra segment register (ES).

If your program has a constant CS, DS, and SS, then you could have as much as 64K of code, 64K of data, and 64K of stack. Even though the address width is 20 bits, the most significant (leftmost) four bits are constant, so the maximum size of each segment is 64K. If your program is smart enough to use ES for other data, then the total program size can be as big as 256K. This size, of course, is somewhat less than the 1-megabyte range afforded by the 20-bit address width.

To allow the code in a program to occupy more than 64K, the microprocessors include jump and call instructions that contain a new segment address in their operands. The CS register is loaded with the new segment value, and the jump or call then proceeds to the address offset from that new value. In the case of a call, the old segment value is pushed on the stack along with the code offset address of the instruction following the call. A special return instruction pops the calling segment address as well as the calling offset to effect a return. These operations are called **long** jumps, calls, and returns, and are contrasted to the **near** jumps, calls, and returns that assume a constant CS register value.

To allow the data in a program to exceed 64K, the program must set the DS (or ES) register to the address of one of several 64K segments and then refer to offsets from that segment address. This process must be done each time the program wants to refer to data in a segment other than the most current one.

These operations are mostly transparent to the C programmer. You will need to understand how they work if you integrate C and assembly language functions, but most programmers can ignore these functions most of the time. You must understand that a large data model program has a pointer size that is different from that of an integer, and that, likewise, a large code model has a function pointer size that is not the same as an integer. Large data and code pointers are not simply 32-bit integral values. They are represented as segment:offset pairs of 16-bit values. The old rules that allowed you to mix integers and pointers are no longer valid. Such cavalier programming is out of fashion; the two types are no longer indistinguishable.

Most programs can be written within 64K of code and 64K of data. Certainly, you can cite examples of programs that cannot be written as such, but most can. Witness the success of several compilers that cannot support any but the "small" memory model. (See the following table.) In fact, you are well advised to restrict as much of your programming as possible to these memory constraints. Programs that have more than 64K of code or data must pay a toll in execution performance as well as memory space. It takes instruction cycles to pass those segment addresses from function to function and to load their values into the registers.

When a program is too large for the so-called "small" memory model, the programmer needs a compiler that will support one of the large code or data memory models. There are four acknowledged models and several extensions. Their names differ among the compilers, but their characterisics are the same:

Model	Code	Data
Small	64K	64K
Large Data	64K	1 Meg
Large Code	1 Meg	64K
Large	1 Meg	1 Meg

There is also a "tiny" model that restricts all code and data to a total of 64K. This model corresponds to the DOS format for .COM-executable files. Many compilers do not support this model, but the Mix C Compiler supports only the tiny model.

Usually, even in a large data model, individual arrays cannot exceed 64K, and individual dynamic heap memory allocations are restricted to 64K. Similarly, the stack is usually restricted to 64K.

Some of the extensions allow for partitioning of data into initialized external data, uninitialized external data, and the dynamic heap from which memory is allocated. This partitioning allows you to tailor your memory model to the precise requirements of the program while preserving the processing efficiency of the small model for the rest of the program. Other extensions provide for individual data structures that exceed the usual 64K limit.

Some compilers allow memory models to be mixed in the same program. Code segments compiled under one model can be linked with those compiled under a different compiler. Other compilers do not allow this linkage. Some of these compilers will warn you when you link modules; others blithely link the modules, building a program that goes off in the weeds when you try to run it.

You must know about memory models, because you must know how to compile and link them when they are needed. The compilers that support multiple models usually default to the small model, and their tutorial examples (which always tell you how to compile and link "hello, world") stick to the default. The examples in this book all work with the small model, and the command files in this chapter that build the programs assume that model. If you use the libraries with application programs that need a different model, you must rebuild them accordingly.

Object Librarians

As the linker program builds an executable module, it reads object modules from two kinds of files: the object files that are the direct output from the compiler and files that contain many object files, usually from earlier compiles. These files are called **object libraries**, and the utility programs that manage them are called **object librarians**.

An object librarian program is used to add, delete, replace, and extract object modules in object library files. Such a program is necessary in any development environment that employs reusable software functions. Since reusable software functions are the premise of the Cdata DBMS and one of the lessons of this book, you may assume that a librarian is critical to the approach.

The compilers all provide their standard libraries (as well as special-purpose libraries) in object library files, but they do not all provide object librarian programs. If your compiler supports the DOS LINK format, and you have the Microsoft Macro Assembler, MASM, then the librarian program, LIB.EXE, that comes with MASM can be used. Other librarian programs are available from third-party vendors, but, if you are considering the cost of a compiler that does not include a librarian, you better add the cost of one to your budget.

Editors

You use an **editor** program to enter source code into a file so that you can compile the program. There are many such programs, and some compilers include an editor either as standard equipment or as an option.

It is not important that an editor be included with the compiler. Certainly, having an editor is important, but you are not required to use the one, if any, that your compiler vendor provides. It's OK if you do, but it is not that important.

A preference for an editor — the features it provides and the way it provides them — is a personal choice. Like politics and religion, your preferences are your own business, no one else's, and the point is not to influence you here.

You can get editors from many places. Some excellent ones are available free of charge through the graces of Public Domain software. Usually, their source code is included, and usually they are written in C. Most Bulletin Board Services, particularly those with a C language orientation, contain several such free editor programs, which can be yours for the cost of a phone call.

A new generation of programmer's editors is emerging. These editors have a macro language that lets you write macros that can be invoked from any keystroke. You can program them to emulate other editors and word processors, and you can build in some amount of context intelligence to help you code. For example, you can make them sensitive to the braces and indentation conventions of the C language.

The old editors displayed one line at a time and would work with only one file at a time. The new editors allow full-screen processing of multiple source files in multiple video windows.

Future compilers will have editors integrated into their software development environments (as does Turbo C now). You can be sure that these environments will include two other editor features. First, you will be able to customize the editor, and second, you will be able to substitute a different editor of your own choosing. A compiler that forces you to use its editor will not survive.

Make Utilities

Make is a programmer's productivity utility program and is one of those tools that becomes indispensable as soon as you've used it the first time. Compiling and linking an application software system is described in a control file that the make program uses to rebuild your system whenever you have changed something.

Make is much more than a batch file that recompiles and relinks everything. Make deals with "rules" that tell it how object files depend on source files, libraries depend on object files, and executable programs depend on libraries and other object files. These dependencies are recorded in a **makefile** that the make program reads. Then, when you run make, those source files that are newer than their object files are recompiled; those libraries that are older than any of the object files that should be in them are rebuilt, and those executable files that are older than their object files and the libraries they use are relinked. This process is recursive; if make builds as a target a file that is a dependent of another target, the other target is built also — even if it appears ahead of the original target in the makefile.

Using make means that you can change several source files (including headers) over a period of time for a system that is composed of hundreds of programs. While doing so, you don't need to bother keeping track of which files you changed. You then run the make program. It automatically rebuilds the system, compiling and linking only the files that need it.

Make uses the current system date and time and the date and time that is stamped on a file to decide which file is older and which is newer. It then uses a command file (called the **makefile**) to see what to compare and what to do if a comparision shows that a dependent file should be rebuilt.

The usual format for a makefile entry follows this pattern:

```
target file: dependent file(s)
    command line
```

The target file is a file to be built if any of the dependent files is newer than the target file. The command line is the DOS command that will be executed if the target file is to be rebuilt.

An entry to compile a program might resemble the following:

```
btree.obj: btree.c cdata.h
    cc btree
```

Usually, make will set out to make the first target in the file unless you specify a different one on make's command line. A makefile to build a system that consists of a large number of targets will have a dummy target and command as the first entry, with the target list (usually all the .EXE files) as the dependents.

Some make programs allow you to encode macro strings to avoid repetitious link statements and dependencies. Some have built-in rules that already know the relationship between two kinds of files, for example, a .C file and a .OBJ file.

Make can be used for processes other than compiling and linking, but where actions can be dependent on the respective time stamps of files. For example, make can be used to manage the backups of large source code libraries. Following is how a typical entry would be coded:

```
b:btree.c: btree.c
    copy btree.c b:
```

If the file on the default drive is newer than the same file on the b: drive, the copy command is executed. In this case, the make utility must understand the difference between the two colons on the first line.

Some compilers include a make utility as standard equipment. Others support a mini-make in their "one-liner" compiler driver programs (discussed later in this chapater). Several make programs are available commercially, and you can find one that can be downloaded from some C language Bulletin Board Systems.

If you aren't already using a make program, you should start using one now. In earlier days, personal computers didn't have clocks, and their operating systems (CP/M, for example) did not record a date/time stamp on disk files. In that environment, make was not possible. Now, with the PC and DOS, make is not only possible, it is necessary. If your computer has no hardware clock/calendar, remember to set your date and time whenever you power up.

Library Source Code

Each compiler includes a standard library of standard functions. To become accepted in the C compiler marketplace, a compiler must include, at a minimum, all the accepted standard functions. Most compilers have additional, nonstandard functions; some so-called standard functions have no standard, and some functions thought to be standard are missing from some compilers, but all compilers have most of the usual functions.

Some compilers include the source code to their libraries and some do not. Some compilers make source code available as an extra-cost option, and some do not offer it at any price.

The value of library source code can be debated. It can provide examples of how to write C code, but only if the code is well-written. Some compiler vendors write many of their library functions in assembly language so that the functions will perform well. Those libraries have limited use as C tutorial material. Others have C code that is best left out of public view.

There is one circumstance where library source code is indispensable — when a library function does not work. If you can show a vendor where the error is in the code, you will get better support for the problem. If you cannot, the vendor will assume that the problem is in your code. If the vendor does not fix an error in a library, you can fix it, but only if you have the source code.

Some vendors worry that users will change the functions, break something, and then call for support. This situation sets up a scenario where the vendor spends time finding out that the problem is not a fault of the product. Support is difficult to provide, and more so if the vendor is supporting the user's code. This situation is often used by vendors as an excuse for not distributing library source code.

It is not good practice to modify functions in the compiler's library merely for the sake of improving their functionality. In doing so, you restrict the portability of your code to the specific site where the modified library is installed. Further, you compromise the value of the vendor's documentation. Other programmers might come behind you, unaware of your modification (having read the compiler's documentation and not yours), and expect the function to work as advertised. A better practice is to rewrite the function and give it a different name. If the compiler's version is available in source code, all the better; you can use it as a basis for your new version. But leave the original function alone.

The occasions where you will see (or make) valid changes to a function in a compiler's function library are few — so few that you can declare the practice off-limits for your programming habits.

The occasions where errors will be found in a compiler's library are more frequent. This book contains code that corrects some of those errors. In these cases, the source code was invaluable in tracing the error.

On one occasion, an error was found in a compiler's **malloc** function. Despite reports to the vendor, the error persists to this day, and the compiler is probably the most popular one on the market. The source code is not provided, and the vendor's response to the problem report was nontechnical, irrelevant, and the vendor refused to acknowledge the error. With that compiler (Microsoft), you should avoid long processes with frequent **mallocs** and **frees** of large blocks of memory. At the time of this book's writing, it still does not work.

One-line Compiler Programs

C is a language that can be compiled in a single pass. The language definition calls for almost every identifier to be declared before it is referenced. The exceptions are statement labels and functions that return integers. References to labels (gotos) are restricted to the functions where the labels are declared. Functions that return integers can be declared implicitly by their initial reference.

A compiler usually passes the source code through several processes. A typical compiler involves a preprocessor, a lexical scan of the source code, a parser, a code generator, an optimizer, an assembler, and a linker. Assemblers and linkers have already been discussed.

The **preprocessor** reads the source code and processes all the **#include**, **#if**, **#define**, and other preprocessor statements. The output from this pass is piped to the **lexical scan**, which translates the source code into a file of tokens. The **parser** checks the syntax of the tokens and generates error messages, and the **code generator** compiles the tokens into assembly language. The **optimizer** analyzes the assembly language to see where it can optimize the compiled code to improve module size and execution efficiency. The **assembler** assembles the assembly language into object language, and the **linker** links the object language with the output of other compilations, the libraries, and the startup code.

A single-pass compiler will perform the preprocessor through the optimizer in one pass of the source code file. Often, these compilers generate temporary files of abbreviated tokens that encode the source language and that are passed to the next process. Others will pass each token to the next pass as the token is developed.

Some compilers have a separate program for each of these processes and require you to run each of the programs in succession to compile a program. Others manage everything up to the link process in one program.

Many of the compilers have included a program that allows you to do everything with one command line entry. These programs, called **one-liners**, allow you to name one or more source files, and they compile and link the modules into an executable program. They know the location of the libraries and startup code, so you don't have to name them on the command line. Some of the one-liners allow you to name source files and object files; they will compile only the source files, linking the object files into the executable module. Some allow you to name C source files and assembly language source files as well, picking the correct language processor for each. Some one-liners have a miniature version of the make utility; they will compile a file if its source file is newer than its object module, and they will link a file only if at least one of the object modules is newer than the executable module. These "mini-make" options are not as smart as their big brother counterparts. They are not capable of the complex dependencies and rules that the make program can handle.

One of the compilers, CI-C86, uses a DOS batch file for its one-liner, which executes only the four compilation programs. This approach's drawback is that you can't have another batch file with a series of one-liner invocations because DOS does not allow a batch file to run a series of batch commands. That is why to build the software in this book, the CI-C86 batch file has four lines to compile each program.

Following are discussions of some major C compilers along with their respective tool-building procedures.

AZTEC C

Aztec C, from Manx Software Systems, had its beginnings as a C compiler for the 8080 microcomputer under the CP/M operating system. It enjoyed wide success because it was the first full-language compiler available in that environment, and it worked well. Since then, the Aztec compiler family has grown into a product line that supports different processors and operating systems. An impressive level of compatibility exists among the various compilers so that code developed with one compiler should function predictably when compiled with another.

The Aztec compiler is available in several configurations, each of which adds options at additional cost. The top-of-the-line compiler includes source code for the libraries along with an editor, an assembler, a make utility, a source-level debugger, a librarian, a linker, and a number of useful utilities.

The Aztec editor is named Z and is a version of the vi editor that is used in the UNIX operating system environment.

The documentation is not the best. Manx decided to use a page-numbering scheme that uses mnemonic prefixes (unitools, tech, libov, and so on) that are organized in no sequence at all. Then they decided to put the descriptions of the functions in a sequence that groups like functions under the heading of one of those functions. For example, to find palette() you must look up color(). Functions are further divided into independent functions and DOS-CP/M functions. These two groups are found (if you can find them) far apart from each other. This style persists with each new version of the compiler.

Listing 9.1 (azdbms.bat)

```
rem
rem        azdbms.bat
rem        Build cdata with Aztec C Version 3.40
rem        Compiler is installed in \cc
rem        Cdata source code is in current directory
rem
path \cc
set INCLUDE=\cc
set CLIB=\cc\
cc -dCOMPILER=AZTEC btree
cc -dCOMPILER=AZTEC datafile
cc -dCOMPILER=AZTEC screen
cc -dCOMPILER=AZTEC database
cc -dCOMPILER=AZTEC ellist
cc -dCOMPILER=AZTEC sys
lb ts ellist database screen btree datafile sys
cc -dCOMPILER=AZTEC schema
ln schema.o -lc
schema <cbs.sch >cbs.c1 -1
schema <cbs.sch >cbs.c2 -2
schema <cbs.sch >cbs.c3 -3
cc -dCOMPILER=AZTEC cbs
cc -dCOMPILER=AZTEC qd
cc -dCOMPILER=AZTEC ds
cc -dCOMPILER=AZTEC dblist
cc -dCOMPILER=AZTEC clist
cc -dCOMPILER=AZTEC index
cc -dCOMPILER=AZTEC dbsize
cc -dCOMPILER=AZTEC dbinit
cc -dCOMPILER=AZTEC posttime
cc -dCOMPILER=AZTEC payments
cc -dCOMPILER=AZTEC invoice
ln qd.o cbs.o ts.lib -ls -lc
ln ds.o dblist.o clist.o cbs.o ts.lib -ls -lc
ln index.o cbs.o ts.lib -ls -lc
ln dbsize.o cbs.o ts.lib -ls -lc
ln dbinit.o cbs.o ts.lib -ls -lc
ln posttime.o cbs.o ts.lib -ls -lc
ln payments.o cbs.o ts.lib -ls -lc
ln invoice.o cbs.o ts.lib -lm -ls -lc
```

COMPUTER INNOVATIONS C-86

Computer Innovations C-86 is a C compiler that supports two models, the small model and the large model. It comes with its own librarian (whimsically named "marion") and source code to all the library functions. C86 is distributed on four diskettes, and most of the files are compressed and archived. (The unsqueeze and archive programs are included.) C86 adds up to a sizeable package.

Programs are compiled by four separate programs, and C86 has no one-liner to execute them. A batch file is included that will execute all four passes to compile a program, but this file cannot be called repetitively from an outer batch file; the DOS batch processor does not allow it.

Several C86 constructs are unconventional. There is no **void** function type, and the **gets** function is different from that of the other compilers. (The manual warns you about **gets**, but the problem remains unfixed.) If you code a string constant that has the C comment tokens (/* and */) in it, the compiler treats the tokens and whatever is inside them as a comment, rather than as part of the string. The **atoi** function serves as **atoi** and **atol** as well, and there is no **atol** function. If you declare an external variable and then do not reference it or define it, C86 establishes a phantom reference to it so that the linker thinks the variable is an unresolved symbol. Other compilers just ignore the variable if it is not directly referenced in your code.

Listing 9.2 (cidbms.bat)

```
rem
rem        cidbms.bat
rem        Build cdata with CI C86
rem        Compiler is installed in \c86
rem        link.exe is in \dos
rem        Cdata source code is in current directory
rem
path=\c86;\dos
cc1 -h\c86\ -i -m -dCOMPILER=CI_C86 schema
cc2 schema
cc3 schema
cc4 schema
link schema,schema,,\c86\c86s2s
schema <cbs.sch >cbs.c1 -1
schema <cbs.sch >cbs.c2 -2
schema <cbs.sch >cbs.c3 -3
cc1 -h\c86\ -i -m -dCOMPILER=CI_C86 btree
cc2 btree
cc3 btree
cc4 btree
cc1 -h\c86\ -i -m -dCOMPILER=CI_C86 datafile
cc2 datafile
cc3 datafile
cc4 datafile
cc1 -h\c86\ -i -m -dCOMPILER=CI_C86 screen
cc2 screen
cc3 screen
cc4 screen
cc1 -h\c86\ -i -m -dCOMPILER=CI_C86 database
cc2 database
cc3 database
cc4 database
cc1 -h\c86\ -i -m -dCOMPILER=CI_C86 ellist
cc2 ellist
cc3 ellist
cc4 ellist
cc1 -h\c86\ -i -m -dCOMPILER=CI_C86 sys
cc2 sys
cc3 sys
cc4 sys
```

continued...

...from previous page

```
marion -u ts ellist database screen btree datafile sys
cc1 -h\c86\ -i -m -dCOMPILER=CI_C86 qd
cc2 qd
cc3 qd
cc4 qd
cc1 -h\c86\ -i -m -dCOMPILER=CI_C86 dblist
cc2 dblist
cc3 dblist
cc4 dblist
cc1 -h\c86\ -i -m -dCOMPILER=CI_C86 clist
cc2 clist
cc3 clist
cc4 clist
cc1 -h\c86\ -i -m -dCOMPILER=CI_C86 ds
cc2 ds
cc3 ds
cc4 ds
cc1 -h\c86\ -i -m -dCOMPILER=CI_C86 index
cc2 index
cc3 index
cc4 index
cc1 -h\c86\ -i -m -dCOMPILER=CI_C86 dbsize
cc2 dbsize
cc3 dbsize
cc4 dbsize
cc1 -h\c86\ -i -m -dCOMPILER=CI_C86 dbinit
cc2 dbinit
cc3 dbinit
cc4 dbinit
cc1 -h\c86\ -i -m -dCOMPILER=CI_C86 cbs
cc2 cbs
cc3 cbs
cc4 cbs
cc1 -h\c86\ -i -m -dCOMPILER=CI_C86 posttime
cc2 posttime
cc3 posttime
cc4 posttime
cc1 -h\c86\ -i -m -dCOMPILER=CI_C86 payments
cc2 payments
cc3 payments
```

continued...

...from previous page

```
cc4 payments
cc1 -h\c86\ -i -m -dCOMPILER=CI_C86 invoice
cc2 invoice
cc3 invoice
cc4 invoice
link qd+cbs,,,ts+\c86\c86s2s+\c86\ibmpcs
link ds+dblist+clist+cbs,,,ts+\c86\c86s2s+\c86\ibmpcs
link index+cbs,,,ts+\c86\c86s2s+\c86\ibmpcs
link dbsize+cbs,,,ts+\c86\c86s2s+\c86\ibmpcs
link dbinit+cbs,,,ts+\c86\c86s2s+\c86\ibmpcs
link posttime+cbs,,,ts+\c86\c86s2s+\c86\ibmpcs
link payments+cbs,,,ts+\c86\c86s2s+\c86\ibmpcs
link invoice+cbs,,,ts+\c86\c86s2s+\c86\ibmpcs+\c86\lcms
```

DATALIGHT C

Datalight C is a small, inexpensive package that includes quite a bit for the money. It supports all four of the standard memory models and includes a make utility and source code for the library functions.

Datalight is one of the faster compilers, but the code it generates is among the largest. Datalight does not include its own assembler, linker, librarian, or debugger, although it will support these programs from other vendors.

(Listing 9.3 on next page)

Listing 9.3 (dldbms.bat)

```
rem        dldbms.bat
rem        Build cdata with Datalight C
rem        Compiler is installed in \bin, \include, \lib
rem        Link.exe is in \dos
rem        Cdata source code is in current directory
rem
set path=\bin;\dos
set INCLUDE=\include
set TMP=c:\
set LIB=\lib
dlc -dCOMPILER=DATALIGHT -c btree.c
dlc -dCOMPILER=DATALIGHT -c datafile.c
dlc -dCOMPILER=DATALIGHT -c screen.c
dlc -dCOMPILER=DATALIGHT -c database.c
dlc -dCOMPILER=DATALIGHT -c ellist.c
dlc -dCOMPILER=DATALIGHT -c sys.c
dlc -dCOMPILER=DATALIGHT schema.c
schema <cbs.sch >cbs.c1 -1
schema <cbs.sch >cbs.c2 -2
schema <cbs.sch >cbs.c3 -3
dlc -dCOMPILER=DATALIGHT qd.c cbs.c ellist.obj database.obj
                        screen.obj btree.obj datafile.obj
                        sys.obj
dlc -dCOMPILER=DATALIGHT ds.c dblist.c clist.c cbs.obj
                        ellist.obj database.obj btree.obj
                        datafile.obj sys.obj
dlc -dCOMPILER=DATALIGHT index.c cbs.obj database.obj
                        btree.obj datafile.obj sys.obj
dlc -dCOMPILER=DATALIGHT dbsize.c cbs.obj database.obj
                        datafile.obj btree.obj sys.obj
dlc -dCOMPILER=DATALIGHT dbinit.c cbs.obj database.obj
                        btree.obj datafile.obj sys.obj
dlc -dCOMPILER=DATALIGHT posttime.c cbs.obj database.obj
                        screen.obj btree.obj datafile.obj
                        sys.obj
dlc -dCOMPILER=DATALIGHT payments.c cbs.obj database.obj
                        screen.obj btree.obj datafile.obj
                        sys.obj
dlc -dCOMPILER=DATALIGHT invoice.c cbs.obj database.obj
                        btree.obj datafile.obj sys.obj
```

DeSmet C

DeSmet C is one of the early C compilers for the PC. This compiler has a large and loyal following, and much public domain software has been developed with it.

Version 2.4 is the DeSmet C version that was available for this project. This version lacks some of the more recent improvements to the language, among them the new structure member naming rules. This absence prevented the use of DeSmet C for the Cdata software. But for that omission, DeSmet C could still be used in this work.

DeSmet C includes an editor named **SEE**. It is a single-window programmer's editor with sufficient features to support most programming projects. The source code for the editor is available, but its value is questionable. DeSmet C permits many nonportable constructs, and the SEE code uses most of them, making SEE a shining example of nonportable code. Unless you are going to compile it with DeSmet C exclusively, the use of the SEE source code is not advised.

DeSmet C supports the small memory model and comes with its own assembler, linker, and librarian. Its assembly language is similar to but still different from standard IBM or Microsoft assembly language.

DeSmet offers a debugger and a make utility as options. Library source code is not included.

ECO-C88

Eco-C88 is an inexpensive, small model compiler that has been on the market for several years. Eco-C88 has taken some bum raps in the popular technical media, and the reasons for this criticism are not clear. The compiler works well and as advertised, and the vendor, Ecosoft, supports it with frequent upgrades and a commitment to the emerging ANSI standard.

Eco-C88 has a one-liner compile and link program that includes a mini-make. Ecosoft also gives you the source code to this program.

Eco-C88 has no assembler, linker, or librarian of its own. An editor is available as an option.

Although the compiler's documentation is small and terse, it is adequate. More detail could be offered about the library functions, and Ecosoft could remove the overly general statement that virtually all reported bugs have been in the programmer's code rather than in the compiler. A bug was reported, and Ecosoft acknowledged it, fixed it, and sent a free upgrade. That reponse was nice, but the claim appeared unchanged in the next version of the Eco-C88 manual. Such an attitude from Ecosoft might account for their lack of favor with magazine reviewers.

Listing 9.4 (ecdbms.bat)

```
rem
rem        ecdbms.bat
rem        Build cdata with Eco-C88
rem        Compiler is installed in \bin and \headers
rem        link.exe is in \dos
rem        Cdata source code is in current directory
rem
path=\bin;\dos
set INCLUDE=\headers
cc -dCOMPILER=ECOC -m schema
schema <cbs.sch >cbs.c1 -1
schema <cbs.sch >cbs.c2 -2
schema <cbs.sch >cbs.c3 -3
cc -dCOMPILER=ECOC -m qd cbs ellist database screen btree
                datafile sys
cc -dCOMPILER=ECOC -m ds dblist clist cbs ellist database
                btree datafile sys
cc -dCOMPILER=ECOC -m index cbs database btree datafile sys
cc -dCOMPILER=ECOC -m dbsize cbs database btree datafile sys
cc -dCOMPILER=ECOC -m dbinit cbs database btree datafile sys
cc -dCOMPILER=ECOC -m posttime cbs screen database btree
                datafile sys
cc -dCOMPILER=ECOC -m payments cbs screen database btree
                datafile sys
cc -dCOMPILER=ECOC -m invoice cbs database btree datafile sys
```

HIGH C

High C is a powerful, full-featured compiler system that is part of a larger language development environment. Its implementation of the C language complies with the emerging ANSI standard.

High C takes a long time to compile a program, which is probably because of its position in a language development environment that supports other languages and the extent of the optimization that High C performs.

The executable programs generated by High C are more efficient (smaller, faster) than most of the other compilers. The best use of High C is for the final compile. You can use one of the fast compilers for software development, and then compile the final program with High C. Some programming projects go on forever, however, and in those cases, this suggestion would not work; you would always be changing and recompiling.

The High C standard library omits the unbuffered input/output functions (**open**, **close**, **read**, **write**, **lseek**). No doubt these are conscious omissions since the ANSI standard also omits them. But the Cdata programs use the missing functions; therefore, a procedure for building the software with High C is not included in this chapter. The software does, however, operate correctly with High C if you make the necessary substitutions of **fopen**, **fclose**, **fread**, **fwrite**, and **fseek** for the missing functions. You must substitute the FILE pointer for the integer device handle and provide a substitution for the **ci()** function in **sys.c** to manage keyboard input without echo.

LATTICE C

Lattice C is the old-timer among IBM PC compilers. Its origins go back to the earliest days of the PC, and it is a reliable and mature product. Lattice does not have the zippy performance of the newer compilers, but it is respectable.

The first Microsoft C compiler was really the Lattice compiler in a Microsoft binder. When Microsoft developed their own C compiler, they aimed for a measure of compatibility with the Lattice compiler to ease the conversion problems their users would experience, so a high degree of compatibility still exists between the two compilers.

Lattice does not include the source code for the compiler's library, and they expect you to use the standard DOS linker. They include a one-liner compile program that provides a librarian and a mini-make operation. Lattice has a make utility program and a source level debugger that can both be purchased separately.

Listing 9.5 (lcdbms.bat)

```
rem
rem        lcdbms.bat
rem        Build cdata with Lattice C Version 3.2
rem        Compiler is installed in its default configuration
rem        link.exe is in \dos
rem        Cdata source code is in current directory
rem
path=\lc;\dos
set include=\lc
lc -dCOMPILER=LATTICE -L -M -n schema
schema <cbs.sch >cbs.c1 -1
schema <cbs.sch >cbs.c2 -2
schema <cbs.sch >cbs.c3 -3
lc -dCOMPILER=LATTICE -M -n -Rts ellist database screen btree
                  datafile sys
lc -dCOMPILER=LATTICE -L+ts -M -n qd cbs
lc -dCOMPILER=LATTICE -L+ts -M -n ds dblist clist cbs
lc -dCOMPILER=LATTICE -L+ts -M -n dbsize cbs
lc -dCOMPILER=LATTICE -L+ts -M -n index cbs
lc -dCOMPILER=LATTICE -L+ts -M -n dbinit cbs
lc -dCOMPILER=LATTICE -L+ts -M -n posttime cbs
lc -dCOMPILER=LATTICE -L+ts -M -n payments cbs
lc -dCOMPILER=LATTICE -Lm+ts -M -n invoice cbs
```

LET'S C

Let's C is in this chapter because the author won a copy of it in a promotional contest run by Mark Williams Company. For 25 words or less, Let's C became a part of the Cdata compiler inventory. The compiler is a small model subset of the larger compiler environment that is available from Mark William's Company. It is an inexpensive compiler that performs well.

Let's C includes a version of the editor named EMACS that has been popular on mini-computers since it was first placed in the public domain. This editor is well known and widely used, so many programmers can adjust to it with little effort.

With Lets C you get a librarian, an assembler, and a linker. The assembler processes a strange dialect of 8086 assembly language. The one-liner compiler processes the program all the way through the linker.

You cannot link Let's C programs with libraries in the standard DOS format since Let's C uses its own object file format. To get this capability, you must upgrade to the bigger, more expensive Mark William's C Compiler.

(Listing 9.6 on next page)

Listing 9.6 (ltdbms.bat)

```
rem
rem         ltdbms.bat
rem         Build cdata with Let's C
rem         Compiler is installed in \bin
rem         Cdata source code is in current directory
rem
path=\bin
set CCHEAD=-xl\bin\ -xc\bin\
cc -dCOMPILER=LETSC -c btree.c
cc -dCOMPILER=LETSC -c datafile.c
cc -dCOMPILER=LETSC -c screen.c
cc -dCOMPILER=LETSC -c database.c
cc -dCOMPILER=LETSC -c ellist.c
cc -dCOMPILER=LETSC -c sys.c
lb c ts.olb
lb r ts.olb ellist.o database.o screen.o btree.o datafile.o
        sys.o
cc -dCOMPILER=LETSC schema.c
schema <cbs.sch >cbs.c1 -1
schema <cbs.sch >cbs.c2 -2
schema <cbs.sch >cbs.c3 -3
cc -dCOMPILER=LETSC qd.c cbs.c ts.olb
cc -dCOMPILER=LETSC ds.c dblist.c clist.c cbs.o ts.olb
cc -dCOMPILER=LETSC index.c cbs.o ts.olb
cc -dCOMPILER=LETSC dbsize.c cbs.o ts.olb
cc -dCOMPILER=LETSC dbinit.c cbs.o ts.olb
cc -dCOMPILER=LETSC posttime.c cbs.o ts.olb
cc -dCOMPILER=LETSC payments.c cbs.o ts.olb
cc -dCOMPILER=LETSC -f invoice.c cbs.o ts.olb
```

MICROSOFT C

Microsoft C is the compiler to be reckoned with. It is probably the most successful C compiler for the IBM PC, and its success is easily accounted for. Microsoft C is the product of the leader among microcomputer language developers. That fact alone would guarantee it a measure of acceptance. But, besides the product name, Microsoft C has three distinctive advantages over its competition. First, it still works, and it always has worked. Microsoft C, in its first release (the Microsoft product, not the Lattice compiler that Microsoft sold under its own label for a while), was as dependable as most compilers are after years on the market. Second, it clearly has the best documentation of any other compiler available today. Third, it has Codeview.

Codeview is the showcase source-level debugger that appeared as standard equipment when Microsoft released version 4.0 of the C compiler. Codeview is a book in itself. No other debugger comes close.

The Microsoft C compiler includes a librarian and a linker, but no assembler or editor. The source code for the library is unavailable.

A make utility is included but is not as comprehensive as those available with other compilers; however, it works. The make utility occasionally reports "not enough core," indicating that it was adapted from a mini or main-frame computer. (Microcomputers do not have core; they have RAM.)

(Listing 9.7 on next page)

Listing 9.7 (msdbms.bat)

```
rem
rem        msdbms.bat
rem        Build cdata with Microsoft C Version 4
rem        Compiler is installed in \ms
rem        Compiler .h files are in \include
rem        Compiler libraries are in \lib
rem        Cdata source code is in current directory
rem
path=\ms
set INCLUDE=\include
set LIB=\lib
set TMP=\test
cl -c -DCOMPILER=MICROSOFT btree.c datafile.c screen.c
              database.c ellist.c sys.c
lib ts +ellist+database+screen+btree+datafile+sys;
cl schema.c
schema <cbs.sch >cbs.c1 -1
schema <cbs.sch >cbs.c2 -2
schema <cbs.sch >cbs.c3 -3
cl -DCOMPILER=MICROSOFT qd.c cbs.c -link ts
cl -DCOMPILER=MICROSOFT ds.c dblist.c clist.c cbs.obj -link ts
cl -DCOMPILER=MICROSOFT index.c cbs.obj -link ts
cl -DCOMPILER=MICROSOFT dbsize.c cbs.obj -link ts
cl -DCOMPILER=MICROSOFT dbinit.c cbs.obj -link ts
cl -DCOMPILER=MICROSOFT posttime.c cbs.obj -link ts
cl -DCOMPILER=MICROSOFT payments.c cbs.obj -link ts
cl -DCOMPILER=MICROSOFT invoice.c cbs.obj -link ts
```

MIX C

MIX C is really a book about C that includes a compiler. It is a programmer's learning tool. The price for the package would be a fair price for the manual, which is an excellent tutorial on the C language, complete with comprehensive examples. As a bonus, you get a compiler that you can use to try out the examples.

The MIX C compiler is constrained by its support for only the tiny memory model. This model builds a DOS .COM program with code and data restricted to a total of 64K for the two. This limit severely restricts MIX C as a production-quality compiler. It is, however, more than adequate as the tutorial tool that it is intended to be.

MIX C can be used to build, with some modifications, the software in this book. The use of a **static** function requires that the function be declared as **static** before it is called. This convention is followed by Whitesmith's C compiler and no other. Most compilers generate error messages when you declare a function as **static**. It would confuse the code to have more compiler conditionals, so the MIX C support is not shown in this chapter.

MIX C does not support identifiers that are significant beyond the first 8 characters, so you must change some of the data element names to reflect this limit.

The **ci()** function in **sys.c** should be replaced by the **getch()** function as it has been replaced for several other compilers.

Be wary of the way MIX C returns values from functions. All values are returned on the stack, and the calling function resets the stack when the called function returns. If a called function is not declared in the calling function, the assumption is that it returns an integer, and the compiled code for the calling function will adjust the stack to account for the return of an integer. If the called function returns anything other than an integer (or is a void function), the stack adjustment will be incorrect, and the program will become unpredictable. With most compilers, you can be sloppy about function declaration if you are not going to use what the functions return. Most compilers return values in registers, and those values can be ignored. But with the MIX C compiler, such neglect has its own reward —you will be debugging for a long time.

QC88

QC88 is a hacker's compiler. It implements a healthy subset of the C language (K&R rather than ANSI), runs efficiently, and includes the source code for the library as well as the compiler itself. This last feature is its most valuable benefit. If you are interested in compiler design, QC88 offers a good study in that subject. If, in your software development, you can do without floats, longs, the initialization of automatic variables, the C concept of blocks within functions, **#defines** with parameters, and the improvements offered by the ANSI standard, then QC88 is a good choice. Most programmers would rather not do without those features, and there are enough good compilers that include them. QC88 is unique only because it includes the compiler's source code.

The QC88 package does not include an assembler, linker, editor, or debugger. Since it compiles to assembly language source code, you must have a Microsoft, IBM, or compatible assembler before you can develop any programs with QC88.

The software in this book does not compile with QC88 because most of the missing features are used in the Cdata functions or the example programs. It would be a significant effort to modify the code for QC88, but it is possible.

Once again, the strength of QC88 is in the compiler source code that is included. You can learn a lot about compilers by playing with QC88's code. You can learn a lot about programmming, too, because QC88 itself is a good example of C language programming.

TURBO C

Turbo C is more than a compiler; it is a programming environment with an integrated editor. The editor can be configured to the programmer's keyboard preferences, and the system includes context-sensitive on-line help and error messages. Besides those features, Turbo C is the fastest compiler available for the PC.

Turbo C can be run in two configurations. The first is the command line mode that is similar to that of the other compilers. The second is called the **Turbo C Integrated Development Environment**, which integrates the compiler with the editor and allows interactive program creation, modification, compilation, and execution, all under the control of a window and menu environment. A make utility is available in either the command line mode or the Integrated Development Environment. The assembler is internal to the compiler, and assembly language functions must be assembled with the Microsoft or IBM assembler; however, assembly language statements can be inserted into the C program with a special Turbo C keyword, **asm**.

Turbo C reflects its origin. Borland is the premier software vendor of memory resident programs, and Turbo C includes functions that support the development of memory resident programs. For a detailed study of this and other advanced uses of Turbo C, refer to *Turbo C: Memory Resident Utilities, Screen I\O and Programming Techniques* (also by the author, MIS:Press, Publication date: Fall 1987).

(Listing 9.8 on next page)

Listing 9.8 (tcdbms.bat)

```
rem
rem        tcdbms.bat
rem        Build cdata with Turbo C
rem        Compiler is installed in \tc
rem        Cdata source code is in current directory
rem
path=\tc
tcc -DCOMPILER=TURBOC schema
schema <cbs.sch >cbs.c1 -1
schema <cbs.sch >cbs.c2 -2
schema <cbs.sch >cbs.c3 -3
tcc -DCOMPILER=TURBOC qd.c cbs.c ellist.c database.c
                      screen.c btree.c datafile.c sys.c
tcc -DCOMPILER=TURBOC ds.c dblist.c clist.c cbs.obj
                      ellist.obj database.obj btree.obj
                      datafile.obj sys.obj
tcc -DCOMPILER=TURBOC index.c cbs.obj database.obj btree.obj
                      datafile.obj sys.obj
tcc -DCOMPILER=TURBOC dbsize.c cbs.obj database.obj
                      datafile.obj btree.obj sys.obj
tcc -DCOMPILER=TURBOC dbinit.c cbs.obj database.obj btree.obj
                      datafile.obj sys.obj
tcc -DCOMPILER=TURBOC posttime.c cbs.obj database.obj
                      screen.obj btree.obj datafile.obj
                      sys.obj
tcc -DCOMPILER=TURBOC payments.c cbs.obj database.obj
                      screen.obj btree.obj datafile.obj
                      sys.obj
tcc -DCOMPILER=TURBOC invoice.c cbs.obj database.obj btree.obj
                      datafile.obj sys.obj
```

WHITESMITH'S C

Whitesmith's C is a big, professional compiler. Its documentation is in two slip binders that are three inches wide each and packed with plenty of information.

Whitesmith's C can be installed with one of two libraries: the ANSI C Runtime library or the Whitesmith's C library. Both libraries can be supplemented with the Common library. The purpose for these library definitions is to allow the developer to choose the environment with which the software is to be compatible — the ANSI environment, the ANSI environment with extensions, or the environment that was supported by older Whitesmith's compilers. Whitesmith supports compilers for many different micro, mini, and mainframe computers, and they strive for portability among all their compilers.

The biggest drawback to Whitesmith's C is its performance. Like High C, Whitesmith's takes a long time to compile and a link a program.

Whitesmith's omitted the **creat** function, and it has the same unconventional treatment of **static** functions that was found with the MIX C compiler. (How odd that the two compilers with this characteristic are the most and least expensive of all the compilers tested.) Because of these two problems, the Whitesmith's compiler cannot be used to compile the Cdata code as published in this book; however, the code has been successfully modified to use the Whitesmith's compiler. The modifications include **static** function declarations before the functions are called and the substitution of the **create** function in the Whitesmith's library for the missing **creat** function.

Whitesmith's has no way to execute interrupts other than the DOS interrupt 21. For this reason, you are forced to use the ANSI.SYS protocols that are published in this book; you cannot improve performance with low-level BIOS interrupt calls.

WIZARD C

Wizard C has been judged by one reviewer as the "best" C compiler available. The basis for that judgement is not clear, given the large selection of excellent products, but Wizard C is certainly among the best. It supports all four memory models (plus two others) and is distributed with library source code, a one-liner, and a lint utility. **Lint** is a UNIX program that tests C source files for consistency, correctness, and isolates likely programming and portability problems. Wizard allows you to specify lint checking as a function of the one-liner compile and link process.

As reported above, the Wizard **strncmp** function is not the standard implementation. Other than that difference, no problems were encountered in compiling the Cdata programs with Wizard C.

Wizard C is one of the fastest of the compilers and compiles programs that are among the smallest in object file size.

Listing 9.9 (wzdbms.bat)

```
rem
rem        wzdbms.bat
rem        Build cdata with Wizard C
rem        Compiler is installed in \bin
rem        Compiler .h and library files defined in wizard.cfg
rem        Link.exe is in \dos
rem        Cdata source code is in current directory
rem
path=\bin;\dos
cc -DCOMPILER=WIZARD -c btree.c
cc -DCOMPILER=WIZARD -c datafile.c
cc -DCOMPILER=WIZARD -c screen.c
cc -DCOMPILER=WIZARD -c database.c
cc -DCOMPILER=WIZARD -c ellist.c
cc -DCOMPILER=WIZARD -c sys.c
cc -DCOMPILER=WIZARD schema.c
schema <cbs.sch >cbs.c1 -1
schema <cbs.sch >cbs.c2 -2
schema <cbs.sch >cbs.c3 -3
cc -DCOMPILER=WIZARD qd.c cbs.c ellist.obj database.obj
                     screen.obj btree.obj datafile.obj sys.obj
cc -DCOMPILER=WIZARD ds.c dblist.c clist.c cbs.obj ellist.obj
                     database.obj btree.obj datafile.obj
                     sys.obj
cc -DCOMPILER=WIZARD index.c cbs.obj database.obj btree.obj
                     datafile.obj sys.obj
cc -DCOMPILER=WIZARD dbsize.c cbs.obj database.obj
                     datafile.obj btree.obj sys.obj
cc -DCOMPILER=WIZARD dbinit.c cbs.obj database.obj btree.obj
                     datafile.obj sys.obj
cc -DCOMPILER=WIZARD posttime.c cbs.obj database.obj
                     screen.obj btree.obj datafile.obj sys.obj
cc -DCOMPILER=WIZARD payments.c cbs.obj database.obj
                     screen.obj btree.obj datafile.obj sys.obj
cc -DCOMPILER=WIZARD invoice.c cbs.obj database.obj btree.obj
                     datafile.obj sys.obj
```

SUMMARY

With one of these compilers and the source code taken from this book, you can build a usable and effective data base management system. These Cdata functions are similar in form and purpose to the ones that underpin the most complex commercial data base manager. The rich compiler resource spawned by the PC industry makes it possible to implement these tools in the personal computer environment in a manner that is fast, easy, inexpensive, and fun.

EPILOGUE

The construction of a data base management system is a significant undertaking. The software in this book was developed over the period of several years and was the result of necessity. The first major hurdle was in the comprehension of the need for the software. When a need clearly exists, it is not always clear what the need is. As a result, such needs are not always filled immediately; they grow in increments as they are defined. As the lessons of a project's development are learned, its own evolution is modified; the solution alters the problem. If the solution takes long enough, the problem can become completely changed by the effects of such prolonged attention.

The problems addressed by this book are not new. These solutions are not so much new as they are different and only recently available in the data base and PC environments. By acquiring the lessons and examples contained in this book, you gain another way of looking at old problems.

The concepts presented in this work are bound only by your imagination and creativity. Each of us finds new ways to solve problems by using and improving solutions that others have found and shared. This body of technical knowledge will grow as explorations widen and people share their findings. Knowledge is freedom, and skill and ability are the products of knowledge placed into practice. Through the sharing of ideas, discoveries, successes, and failures, you can broaden the knowledge base. As you learn and use new techniques, you will change and improve them, and those techniques will evolve. If you share these new ideas with others, you will change how things are done, and something good is bound to come of it.

INDEX

C

D

ds.c, 210, 211
Duncan, Ray, 3
D__BOF, 127, 128
D__DUPL, 125, 129
D__EOF, 127, 128, 130
D__NF, 125, 126, 129
D__PRIOR, 129

E

ecdbms.bat, 283
Eco-C88, 6, 258, 260, 283
Ecosoft, 258
edit, 218
editor, 269
ellen, 75
ellist, 215
ellist.c, 216
elmask, 77
eltype, 77
EMACS, 287
epos, 132
errno.h, 259

F

fclose, 285
fcntl.h, 259
fhdr, 118
FILE, 285
file specifications, 92
filename, 215, 238
files, 39
file__close, 156
file__create, 156
file__ele, 81
file__open, 156
find__rcd, 125
firstkey, 185
first__rcd, 126
first__record, 118

K

key data elements, 19
key index, 44
key retrievals, 41
keyboard, 187
keys.h, 187, 188
keyval, 186

L

labels, 274
lastkey, 186
last__rcd, 127
Lattice, 258
Lattice C, 6, 258, 259, 260, 285, 289
lcdbms.bat, 286
Let's C, 6, 258, 259, 260, 287
lexical scan, 274
LIB.EXE, 269
LINK.EXE, 263
linker, 263, 274
lint, 296
locate, 185
lseek, 285
ltdbms.bat, 288

M

make, 270
malloc, 274
Manx Software Systems, 258, 276
many-to-many, 21, 46, 58, 78
many-to-one, 21
Marion the librarian, 278
Mark Williams Company, 258, 287
Martin, James, 59
MASM, 269
MAXELE, 93
MAXFILS, 93
MAXINDEX, 93

MAXKEYLEN, 93
McCreight, E., 119
memory models, 262, 266
Microsoft, 258, 265
Microsoft C, 6, 258, 259, 274, 286, 289
Microsoft Windows, 189
Mix C, 7, 267
MIX C, 291, 295
MOVE CORRESPONDING, 131
msdbms.bat, 290
multiple-file retrievals, 44, 47

N

name__cvt, 239
network data base, 56
network data model, 55
new__record, 157
nextkey, 186
next__rcd, 117, 127
NODE, 93, 121
Norton, Peter, 3

O

object librarians, 268
one-to-many, 21, 46
one-to-one, 21, 46
open, 259, 260, 285
OPENMODE, 259
operating systems, 4
optimizer, 274

P

parser, 274
Pascal, 66
payments.c, 217, 252, 253
PC-DOS, 4
performance requirements, 35

posttime.c, 217, 249, 250
precedence of a query expression, 43
preprocessor, 274
prevkey, 186
prev__rcd, 128
primary key, 19, 45, 92
printf, 117, 265
problem definition, 72
problem specification, 32
PROJENTR.BAT, 245
PROJREPT.BAT, 246
protect, 218
putchar, 189
put__char, 189
put__field, 219
put__record, 158

Q

QC88, 7, 263, 292
qd.c, 200, 204
queries, 41

R

range searches, 42
rcd__fill, 131
read, 285
record lengths, 17
relational data base, 10, 57, 58
relational data model, 18, 55, 119
relationships, files, 21
reports, 44
resource list, 33
retrieval paths, 47
retrievals, 41
rlen, 133
ROM BIOS, 189
RPTR, 93, 118, 157
rtn__rcd, 129

S

scanning data files, 44
schema, 4, 17, 48, 64
schema compiler, 5
schema.c, 98, 99, 117, 259
screen.c, 217, 220, 261
secondary keys, 20, 92
SEE, 283
seqrcd, 130
significance of identifiers, 16, 67
sizeof, 133
stat.h, 259
static, 291, 295
stderr, 111
stdin, 111
stdio.h, 116
stdout, 111, 115
strncmp, 260, 296
strongly typed languages, 67
structure member names, 283
structure member names, 67
sys.c, 189, 190, 259, 261, 285, 291

T

tally, 219
tcdbms.bat, 294
treenode, 121
Turbo C, 6, 258, 259, 270, 292
TurboDos, 4
typedef, 118, 157
types.h, 259

U

UNIX, 276, 296
utility functions, 5
utility programs, 61

V

verify__rcd, 126
vi, 276
void, 260, 278

W

Whelan's chops, 8, 240
Whitesmiths C, 7, 291, 295
Wizard C, 6, 258, 260, 296
Wizard Systems, 258
write, 285
wzdbms.bat, 297

Z

Z, 276

__iomode, 260